Christine Brown

THE VISITS

Limited Special Edition. No. 16 of 25 Paperbacks

Christine Brown has worked on local and national newspapers and has written *Goodbye Patrick*, the story of her five adopted children. She read English at St Hilda's College, Oxford, and gained her PhD on the Catholic Novel at Reading University in 2004. She was born in Edinburgh and now lives in Buckinghamshire.

Christine Brown

THE VISITS

AUSTIN MACAULEY PUBLISHERS™

LONDON • CAMBRIDGE • NEW YORK • SHARJAH

A CIP catalogue record for this title is available from the British Library.

ISBN 9781528935838 (Paperback)
ISBN 9781528968447 (ePub e-book)

www.austinmacauley.com

First Published (2019)
Austin Macauley Publishers Ltd
25 Canada Square
Canary Wharf
London
E14 5LQ

Prologue

This story tells what it is like for young men in prison and what it was like for an ordinary housewife to hear about it. It does not dwell on the rights and wrongs of the prison system. It simply tells what the men themselves make of it.

I knew nothing of what life inside is like before visiting. I was not influenced by written accounts either by prisoners themselves or prison officers.

Of necessity, the names of the men and the prison I visited have been changed.

Chapter 1

Mark was the first person I visited in prison. Except for his prison number, all I knew about him was his name – Mark. It was some time before I learned his surname. That was all the information I had been given about him, I had no idea what he would be like or what he had done. I didn't know what the inside of prison would be like or how the visit would go. There was no training for this but the odd thing was, I didn't feel at all nervous. It crossed my mind, momentarily, that he might feel nervous since he only knew that he had been allotted an official visitor. So that's how it stood for our first visit. He knew nothing about me and I knew nothing about him. An even playing field in other words so that could work out well, I guessed. The one thought on my mind as I drove towards the prison was this. How would I know what to say to him? What if I couldn't think of anything? What then? Would he want to go back to his cell and leave me, high and dry in the Visits Hall? What a start, failing at the first attempt.

Once through Security, I followed everyone else into the Visits Hall. I paid little attention to what the inside of the prison looked like. I don't know why that was but I thought it better to keep my head down so I passed through security without taking much of it in. I mainly concentrated on how I would start the conversation with someone I didn't know and in an environment completely alien to me. I hadn't reckoned on the hall being so enormous and so crowded. I didn't realise there would be so many officers in attendance. There was a constant hum of noise in the air. That was partly due to the number of young children milling around. There was a surprising number of them as well as adults. I certainly hadn't figured on seeing small children in prison. There were a few infants but most of the children were of school age. I couldn't help wondering how they explained away their absence to school friends and teachers.

The officer at the desk pointed me towards Table 32. I had just sat down when prisoners started coming into the hall in small groups. I watched other visitors waiting, and then exchanging hugs and kisses. I kept my head down since the tables were close together and the greetings close to where I sat were more passionate than I expected. Suddenly, someone said 'hello' and sat down opposite me... I tried pulling my chair in closer, before I realised both table and chairs were bolted down.

My first thought was that he looked so young. I don't know why but I had pictured someone middle aged and maybe older. I learned at our next visit that he had just turned 21. The prison bib covering his sweatshirt made him look even younger. He didn't say anything at all so I reckoned it was down to me and began firing questions at him. So where are you from? Have you been in long? How is it going? Until, luckily for him, I soon ran out of steam which gave him a chance. I learned that he was a young squaddie from Newcastle so he was a long way from home.

He told me he had been in a fight outside a pub where a knife was involved, not his, he assured me. He was charged with Grievous Bodily Harm and given 18 months. Although this was his first time inside, he had already been transferred from another prison near Bristol. So, at least, I had the bare bones of his story.

"I was scared all the time I was in there," he said.
"I had no idea what prison would be like.
There were so many fights. The noise was incredible. I just tried keeping my head down. I didn't know what to expect but this place doesn't seem so bad."

Once he started talking, he just kept going which suited me since I thought that was the way it should go. I didn't want any awkward silences. I could see he was beginning to relax. My questions must have sounded more like an interrogation than a friendly chat. Anyway, I think I had used up my questions. Best just to let him keep going, I thought. He told me a bit about his family. His mother had died in an accident when he was school age. Not long after that, his father took up with someone else and they were now out of touch. He had one brother. I was his first visitor since coming into prison. He spoke very quickly in short, staccato sentences. It wasn't the kind of relaxed chat you would have with a friend, more a filling in of information but, at least, there weren't any awkward silences. The noise in the hall got deafening at times and his accent, Geordie, I think, was hard to pick up. Best, I thought, just to keep listening and smiling.

There was a small tea bar in the hall but he shook his head at my offer of tea and biscuits.

"Just as well," I said, pointing at the queue which had already formed.

Anyway, it was obvious he was keen to talk now that had got started. It sounded as though he had been saving up his conversation.

"You never know who to talk to in here," he explained "I don't want to mix with anyone. I'm trying to keep to myself. I think it's best to keep my head down. I don't want to get pulled into any trouble. It's hard just getting used to the noise on the wings. Someone yells to his mate on another wing so he has to yell back. It gets deafening."

It was the most ordinary conversation but at least it kept going. I was relieved since that had been my main worry. The thought of the two of us sitting there tongue-tied would have been terrible.

He looked more relaxed as the visit went on and even managed the occasional smile. I still couldn't get over how young he looked.

In no time at all, an officer gave us a sign that our time was up. I felt elated that, by my reckoning anyway, it had gone well. I had been told that we were allowed an hour's visiting time. That seemed quite long, given I was spending it with someone I had just met and in a situation new to me. There was nothing too awkward about it and the time had gone quickly. It wasn't a congenial setting with cameras all around, and officers pacing up and down but I still think it had gone well. I was just relieved there weren't any long silences. I can do this, I told myself. In fact I think I could be quite good at it. We rose and shook hands.

"Would you like me to visit next week," I asked.

Just a half smile from him.

"I don't mind," he said.

"At least, it gets me out of my cell."

Chapter 2

My second visit to Mark was quite different. The noise in the visits hall and the feeling of being observed, not just by cameras but by officers, affected me more this time. I suppose this time I was more aware of the place I was in. I had been so keen for the first visit to get under way that these just seemed preliminaries and not very important. I hadn't realised how impersonal and strange it all was until this second visit. I must have gone through it in a kind of trance concentrating on what I was going to say. It was all new to me so I had no idea what to expect but this visit was certainly different. For my first visit, I reckoned I had gone through security in a bit of a daze, since this time, going through, I felt nervous. The body rub down seemed more invasive than I remembered. Unlike at the airport, there was never any eye contact and not a word was said. The sniffer dog, a Labrador, felt heavy as it moved around me. I was used to dogs, having a Labrador of my own, but this was different. I felt a moment of panic and flinched.

"Just keep still," the officer told me.

But it wasn't just the physical part of the security checks which affected me. I got used to that quickly. It was the feeling that once inside the prison system, I seemed to have lost my identity. I don't quite know how that happened. I told myself that was fanciful but in ten years of going through into the hall for a visit I never completely lost that feeling.

I discovered that at each visit, they changed the type of searches. After the rub down, it could be your hair or your mouth which was examined. For my second visit to Mark, it was shoes.

"Shoes," the officer said, without looking at me.

"Oh, right," I said. "I'm one of the official visitors here. I've just started."

I don't know why I volunteered that. I thought it might lighten the atmosphere.

"Shoes," he repeated

Mark looked genuinely pleased to see me on the second visit. He also looked more relaxed. We were two people just having a chat but in an unlikely setting. He told me how the time dragged during lock up.

"I can hardly believe time could go so slowly. You don't think of it when you are on the out. In here, the day just drags. I keep cleaning my cell but that doesn't take much time. They've given me a single cell but I don't know if I have that all the time."

He didn't seem to be a reader which would have put in some time for him. He hoped he might be given some work to do on the wing but had no idea how long that might take.

"I see some guys cleaning the wings. Some of them work in the kitchen. I wouldn't mind what they gave me to do. Anything would help to fill up the time."

Being new to the prison, he didn't have TV in his cell, but that also might come in time.

After a while, if he kept out of trouble, he would be 'enhanced' and allowed one, but until then…

"I think time stands still in here," he said.

He was still locked up for the best part of the day.

"I don't even have a paper to read. That would put in an hour or so."

I learned later I could order a daily newspaper from a local shop and have it sent to him. I thought that would help a bit.

"How about a radio?" I asked him.

I'd heard from somewhere they were provided in cells.

"I don't know about that. Maybe when I'm enhanced. I could get one. I don't know how long that takes. I don't even know if you can ask anyone. Anyway, I wouldn't know who to ask."

Leaving after my second visit, I mentioned the business of radios to one of the officers since I presumed he would be in the know.

"Radios," he said. "Now they want radios. I haven't got a radio."

I found that a bit unlikely but he sounded quite aggrieved so I thought best not to pursue it.

The business of the newspaper was surprisingly easy. I found out there was a newsagent fairly near the prison. I went there on my way home, and explained what I wanted and where I wanted it delivered. He didn't seem surprised and sorted it out quickly.

"They mostly get The Sun in there," he told me

I gave him Mark's prison number and his wing, paid him for a month's supply of the Sun and that was it.

Chapter 3

A prison visitor cannot give a prisoner any personal details, not even their surname. The funny thing is how unimportant that became. It didn't seem to matter since some kind of relationship developed as our visits progress. Mostly, Mark did the talking and I enjoyed listening to him. One-sided though that might have been, somehow, it worked. When he referred to his brother, it was mostly childhood memories so I had the feeling they were not in touch. I think he just wanted to hold on to something from the outside.

"We're best of mates," he assured me. "It's always been like that."

Occasionally, he referred to one or two mates he had on the outside but he didn't seem to hear from anyone and he had no visits. That could just have been a case of out of sight out of mind.

For my part, it was mostly domestic details. I told him about the Labrador I had. It had been a stray which I got from a Rescue centre so it could be unpredictable. I explained how busy the prison car park was and how long I had driven around it.

"Reversing is my weak spot so I look for a couple of spaces together," I told him.

He smiled at that. He smiled a lot. He smiled at anything I told him, although, what he had to smile about was a mystery to me. His life was on hold at the moment and there was nothing he could do about that. There was no point at this stage working out how it would go on when he was released. I didn't want to push him on his future plans, that is, if he had any. Time enough for that since he had an 18-month sentence. I was just glad to see him looking relaxed and avoiding trouble inside. That wasn't too difficult since he was still locked up for long periods. Other official visitors told me how easy it was, especially for first-timers to find themselves in a confrontation not of their making.

"It just takes a couple of them to kick off," I was told. "Something minor can do it, or they might just be bored."

I understood what Mark meant about keeping to himself.

Every now and then, he would assure me, "I start feeling more sure of things – I'm still keeping my head down. I can do this."

Chapter 4

Mark was keen to send his girlfriend a birthday card and asked if I could get one for him. This was the first time he had mentioned a girl friend or asked me to do something for him. This shouldn't be too difficult, I thought.

"What kind of card would you like?"

Mark obviously had some difficulty with that and had to think it over for a while.

"Well, you know, not a soppy one, but a good one. If you could look for one with flowers on it or some kind of a nice picture but nothing too fancy… I don't know really. I'll leave it to you."

"Maybe a bit more than just friendly," I suggested.

"Yes, well, kind of but not too, you know…"

I was getting an idea of what he meant. He still had a long time to serve and anything could happen in that time. I don't know what stage their relationship was at when he was arrested, or if there was a relationship. It could have been something quite casual. Maybe he just wanted some connection with the outside world. I learned later that there is often a fear, especially with long-term prisoners, that friends and family could forget them. Whether something like that was on Mark's mind, I don't know. Anything could happen before his release but the right kind of card with the right kind of message could help.

Choosing that card was trickier than I expected. I felt confident about my local supermarket which had an enormous selection. There were hearts and flowers, and undying love in plenty on their shelves. Choosing one of those would have been easy, but I didn't think undying love was what Mark had in mind. On the other hand, the friendly ones could have been sent to a maiden aunt. I struggled over that. Cards for every relationship conveying every sentiment were there, except what Mark was trying to convey. I toyed with asking one of the assistants but changed my mind. I had an idea what he had in mind. I just wasn't sure I could convey that to the girl at the check-out. I did the best I could, filtering through the different messages and chose one.

It must have done the trick since Mark looked pleased next time I saw him.

"Yes, the card was great. I've already sent it."

I never heard if the message was what this girl wanted to hear. It hadn't been easy choosing it. Still, one thing made it worthwhile. I reckoned I had discovered a gap in the greetings card market.

Chapter 5

Although there was no training given for visiting, one message was loud and clear. You take nothing in and you take nothing out. Anything a visitor tries to take in was considered contraband. A warning notice at the gates of the prison spelled it out. Any visitor caught could face imprisonment. I realised what that was about on my next visit to Mark. Our visits were now going well. We talked quite easily. Even the silences felt comfortable. It all felt relaxed and normal. We were two people just having a chat. The noise, the cameras, the officers pacing around didn't bother either of us anymore. Then an incident in the hall changed that. At least, it gave me a different perspective on how prison could be.

The tables were all reasonably close to each other so while I waited for Mark coming over from the wings, I noticed the girl at the table next to me. It would have been hard not to notice her, since she was blonde, attractive and very skimpily dressed. Once her boyfriend came over, I looked away. These greetings were always more passionate than I wanted to see. Just after Mark got to our table, I was aware of a terrific commotion. The noise was mind-bending since it was happening right next to our table. Officers came running, hurtled towards the prisoner next to us and wrestled him to the ground. Now I could understand why tables and chairs were bolted to the ground. It was the first time I had been close to something so violent. The prisoner struggled and swore but he was quickly pinned down by three officers. A uniformed nurse appeared from nowhere, and he was bundled out of the hall like a huge parcel still swearing and struggling. It had all happened so quickly. The blonde girl, strangely enough, looked unconcerned. She had got to her feet but stood quite still, as though it had nothing to do with her. That seemed unreal. In no time at all, the visiting went on as though nothing had happened.

My heart was thumping. The noise and swearing alone was frightening. It had happened so close to me and was so unexpected I felt really shaken. I had never seen or heard anything like that.

"That was frightening," I said to no one in particular.

I tried sounding unconcerned but I know my voice was shaking.

"I was really scared."

"So was I," Mark said.

I realised he was holding on to my hand.

He had just turned 21. If he had been any younger, he would have been in a Young Offenders Prison. At that moment, he looked very young indeed.

At the next visit, he told me that he and others were strip-searched on the way back to their cells. Random searching was something which could be done frequently. It seemed that the officers already had information that drugs were about to be passed that day.

How they had that information, I don't know. That must have been how it was handled so efficiently. It was something I didn't want to see again. The odd thing was that in no time at all, the hall had returned to normal. I realised, for the first time, what a strange environment I was in weekly for these visits. Maybe regular visitors had seen similar incidents but it was a first for me. The noise, the violence, the way the prisoner was removed like a parcel was something I didn't want to see again. Yet, this had all been watched by young children. How when there were body searches, sniffer dogs and posted warnings, spelling out what the penalties would be could something like that happen. As I learned even with these warnings, mobile phones, the most prized contraband, could be brought in.

I described the experience to one of the long serving visitors, telling him how frightened I had felt.

"You have to remember it's not the real world in here," he told me.

Chapter 6

Choosing a greetings card for Mark had been tricky. Buying him trainers was easy. He had come straight from court into prison so he didn't have much in the way of clothes, in fact, more or less what he was wearing. Some of the men in the visits hall were smartly dressed while others mostly had what the prison handed out – tracksuit bottoms and sweatshirts in a faded maroon shade. Some of the inmates wore elaborate looking trainers and designer tee shirts. The way they were kitted out told you something of the support they had from family and friends. Others were decidedly scruffy. A few of them wore all prison issue. Mark's gear was definitely in the scruffy category. He didn't ask me but I could see his trainers were just holding together.

Once I knew his size, I wandered around the local sports shop to pick out a pair. I had no idea trainers came in such a variety of shapes and colours. Once I told the assistant these were for a friend, shoe size 8, he was keen to show me 'the latest thing'. "A lot of the young guys are going for these," he assured me, producing a pair costing over £50. I decided to have another browse around instead and picked a pair at half that price. I parcelled them up to hand in next time I visited.

I thought that would make our visit shorter since I had to queue at the property dept. with other visitors before going through security. That all took some time. Some visitors had their packages returned to them for one reason or another which meant they had to take them back home again. Fortunately, Mark's trainers went through alright. The contents had to be unwrapped, checked and details, mine and Mark's written down. The good news was that didn't affect the visiting time. We still got an hour together.

Mark was delighted that new trainers were on the way to him. It made me realise how dependent the men were on family support, materially as well as emotionally, once they were inside.

Chapter 7

I had heard there was a chance I could visit through the Prison Chaplaincy instead of the visits hall. This was a concession for official visitors who worked and couldn't manage afternoon visits in the hall. At that time, there were two other visitors taking advantage of this. It meant you could see someone in one of the Chaplaincy offices. The visits there would not only be on a one to one basis, there would be little in the way of interruption. There was no security to go through apart from showing my prison ID when first arriving at the gate. That sounded like a big improvement on hall visits. Mark was happy when I suggested it to him, so six months after our first visit, we met in the Chaplaincy

This was different for both of us. Mark was escorted there by an officer who was bringing a Bible group over to the Chapel. After six months inside, Mark still talked about keeping his head down and avoiding any sign of trouble. For him, visiting through the Chaplaincy would feel a bit more normal, for an hour or so anyway. For my part, I was glad to say goodbye to the sniffer dogs and the body search. Mostly for both of us, it just meant a more normal situation. Well, as normal as anything could be in prison. Sitting in comfortable chairs – not bolted to the ground and surrounded by office paraphernalia, we could have been out in the 'real world', apart, of course, for the bars on the windows. It was a view of sorts which was more than Mark would have from his cell.

Chapter 8

I hadn't paid much attention to Mark's release date. I knew he had already spent some of his sentence in another prison. Our visits were now so comfortable and natural, I never stopped to think when they would end. At our next Chaplaincy visit, Mark gave me a hug before he sat down. He had moved on from the formal handshake. He was about to tell me something. It was good news, by the smile on his face. I thought maybe he had been given a job which would have been good news indeed. That would mean having some time out of his cell. He would be kept occupied for at least part of the day as well as earning a few pounds a week. Not actual cash. No one had cash. Anything prisoners earned by way of jobs went on their 'canteen'. From that, inmates could order some extras, biscuits, coffee or toiletries.

"I've got my date," he said. "I'm going out on a tag."

I couldn't quite take it in what he meant at first.

He was talking about the electronic tag fitted to a prisoner's ankle if he got out before the end of his sentence. It meant being out of prison but having to be at home at certain hours so a trace could be made on a prisoner's movements. Checks could be made on them at any time. I had never considered that for Mark and I don't think he had ever mentioned it. I was so surprised that, for once, I couldn't think what to say.

"So when is that?" I asked.

"Next week, Friday."

That meant this would be our last visit. It had come without warning and hard for me to take on board since coming into prison had become a regular part of my week. Once released, a visitor could have no contact with a prisoner so this really would be goodbye. No more 'see you next week'. It gave me an odd feeling. There hadn't been all that many visits, I suppose, 20 or so in all but they had all gone so well this felt a bit like losing a friend.

"Right," I said. "Well, that's great. You must be so pleased."

I tried to sound animated for him but I didn't feel it.

"Oh, you bet. I can't wait to get home."

Home as I had learned from our talks would be a room in someone else's house. He expected to be sharing that room with his brother.

"So is this accommodation OK? I mean, is it fixed. Is it really somewhere you can stay?"

He obviously wasn't sure, but he still couldn't stop smiling.

"Should be OK," he assured me.

"But you haven't heard from your brother, have you?"

I didn't like bringing him back down to earth, but that sounded vague.

"He's got mates who can put us up, if anything goes wrong."

"Well, that's it, then." I said.

"What?"

"No more visits. What am I going to do on Mondays now?"

He laughed, looking happier than I had ever seen him.

He was so keen just to enjoy the news, I felt mean suggesting things might not be straightforward.

I knew he wouldn't have anyone to meet him at the gate when he left but I couldn't do anything about that. I had seen inmates coming out of the prison gate with their black bags, looking around and then walking towards the main road. Occasionally, I could see one being met by a friend. That was definitely the better option but against the rules for prison visitors.

Mark told me he would be given a train warrant back to Newcastle and about £46 in his hand.

I suggested one or two things he should be thinking about. I reminded him that signing on for benefit as soon as he got home was important. I don't know what he would be like handling money but considering what he would need when he got out, £46 would not last long. He would have to make sure he contacted his probation officer as soon as he got home. I knew he wasn't taking any of this in.

He just wanted to enjoy the moment and I didn't want to spoil that for him. I hadn't expected it to happen so suddenly. I should have spent time discussing things like benefit and probation but there always seemed enough time for that. I hadn't given a thought to the business of tagging or how, suddenly, this would bring visits to an end. I had no idea how he would cope with tagging or any other problems he would have on the outside. There was no way I would ever know. It had been nearly 8 months of visiting him every week. I had seen him change in that time. He had become a bit more confident and relaxed. At least, that was how he was with me. I don't know how he was on the wing. I had no idea how he would be when he found himself suddenly on the outside after being inside for over a year.

He couldn't stop smiling all during the visit. I kept thinking I should be giving him some advice about his release but I know he wouldn't have taken it on board. When time was up, he hugged and held on to me for a minute or two.

"Couldn't have done this without you," he said.

"Oh, I think you could," I laughed.

He just couldn't stop smiling.

Once out of the door leading back to the wings, he turned and waved. He did a silly kind of jig for my benefit and then he disappeared.

Chapter 9

There's a lot of locking and unlocking of gates getting into any prison. For a key holder arriving for a visit, it's fairly straightforward. If you are not a key holder, the downside is waiting for someone to escort you in. As someone who can lose car keys and house keys easily enough, I knew drawing keys was a responsibility too far for me. One of our visitors drove home with his bunch of keys on one occasion and had to drive straight back to the prison. He was horrified at his mistake and was reprimanded for it. Warning enough for me.

When you don't draw keys, that means hanging around until someone has time to come down from the Chaplaincy or there's an officer ready to go through. I never discovered what officers feel about visitors, since my experience is that if they escort you in, they walk briskly ahead of you and say nothing.

My escort, one night, was the Irish nun, Sister Agnes, who, like me, was on her way to the Chaplaincy. I had seen her in a group with the men and was impressed how she handled it. She was obviously popular with them, so I was glad of the chance to have a word with her about that. Going through all these gates takes a bit of time so here was my chance. I just managed to say 'hello' when, as she began to lock and unlock, she pulled a rosary from her pockets and invited me to recite with her. 'Hail Mary, full of grace, the Lord is with thee…' This wasn't what I had in mind. I don't know if the officers locking and unlocking from the other direction were aware of this. Probably not, but. I know she didn't miss a beat, or a Hail Mary until we arrived at the Chaplaincy.

Chapter 10

Once my visits got under way, I began to wish I had made more of the spell I had in the visits centre. It hadn't occurred to me that I would follow that with visiting in the prison. I had never done that kind of work before and I realised early on, I wasn't cut out for it. For a start, I was too slow working out which item cost what and what change was due. Luckily for me, there wasn't a great choice of snacks and since adding up was not my forte, I relied on writing everything down. Check the £10 notes, I was told when I wasn't sure what I was looking for. Each time I held a note up, the customer would give me a stony stare. I couldn't work out why they were all in a rush to be served since there was always a long wait before they could be processed through for their visit. I found it tiring when it was hectic and boring once the centre emptied of customers, since that meant there was nothing for me to do. It was clear that the service industry was not for me but I could have gained something from that kind of volunteering. I realised that my time spent in the centre was part mirror image of what prison was about and I should have taken advantage of that.

I saw young women with small babies come back each week for visits. They mostly looked happy and excited. The older women – and they were in the majority – generally, looked harassed and tired. More than once, I saw a young girl bringing in a new baby to show her partner for the first time. Some brought bulky packages they would have to deposit separately before queuing up for their visit. I saw some who had looked positive when their visits number was called out looking less so when their visit was over.

It wasn't part of my stint as a volunteer in the centre to talk to people and no one ever encouraged it. That was understandable since I was just there selling the refreshments but I wish I had taken more on board when I had the opportunity.

Chapter 11

The men I visited rarely referred to whether they had any visits from family or friends. Once I reflected on the visitors I saw in the centre, that seemed strange. It had given me some insight into both sides of prison life, the men who were doing time and their families holding things together at home. Since, for various reasons, some visits I had were a bit strained, a reference to how a family visit went would have been welcome. Maybe that was because it was personal and they thought it was none of my business. I could only think of one inmate who involved me with his family, but then, he was desperate for some kind of help and was clutching at straws.

Anyway, since so many of them came from broken homes, that could be part of the answer. The inmates I saw might refer to family members at home who 'loved them to bits', but for one reason or another, couldn't visit. I could understand why they kept that part of their prison time separate. Anyway, it was a subject not touched on.

Although I found my stint of serving refreshments to visitors hard going, I was still glad I had that chance of seeing the other side of prison life.

Chapter 12

I had been visiting for a long time before I realised that the prison visitor only has an artificial view of inside, sanitised you could call it. We see very little of violence, for example, so we are protected from anything dangerous. There can be an incident, a prisoner taking his own life, but we rarely hear of it. I only once heard of it from an inmate and once from a Chaplain. I found suicide being described as 'an incident' disturbing enough. We don't see the fights or disturbances which take place on wings. The prisoner in the hall being subdued and removed by officers was handled so quickly that it only had a brief impact on me. I have only once been with a prisoner really distressed by what lay ahead for him.

Apart from a natural sympathy, we might have with a prisoner's predicament that is nothing compared to what a family member or friend must feel on their visit. There must be more disappointments than lights hearted moments. The prison visitor, on the other hand, has more lighthearted moments than you would imagine.

I told one inmate, Vince, during our visit, about the time my house was broken into. His reaction was spontaneous and unexpected. He looked and sounded furious.

"So was mine," he said. "Bloody sauce."

Maybe there's a code between burglars and that had been broken, Omerta, honour amongst thieves, something like that. He certainly looked very annoyed so there was not much I could say. The same went for Vince since he didn't say another word which was unusual for him.

So we both sat there in silence, me thinking about my break-in and Vince thinking about his.

Chapter 13

I hadn't done many visits before something struck me about the stories I was hearing. As my visits went on, the men I saw all seemed to be giving me the same account. I don't mean about their crime since they didn't talk about that and anyway, it wasn't my business to know. It was their family background which word for word was exactly the same in nearly every case. It was as though it came from a script. It was never strong on detail but the facts went like this:

When their parents' marriage got into difficulty, one or other of them left the family home and shortly afterwards, a new partner came in. In each case, it was the dad who left and the mum who brought in someone new. The basic story was the same and the few words that summed it up were the same.

"When my dad left, she brought in the boyfriend. We had a fight about it and before I knew it, that was it. I was out."

None of them blamed the mum, not to me anyway, but the newcomer was usually described to me as 'a tosser, a waste of space'.

In some of the stories I heard, there was a reference to a grandmother who filled the family space, like a surrogate mother. However strong that link was, I wouldn't know but I was always assured that 'she loves me to bits'.

Chapter 14

I thought the phrase 'If you can't do the time, don't do the crime' was a glib kind of mantra with no deep meaning to it. I felt it was conveying a macho message for any inmate who couldn't cut it. Theo, on one of his visits, made me look at it another way. He had just put in what he described as 'the longest weekend in history'.

I understood there were fewer officers on at weekends so the men were locked up longer. If you were lucky enough to have a class to go to, they didn't happen on either Saturday or Sunday. The same applied to jobs. Anything that could break the monotony stopped over the weekend. I was beginning to see what he meant.

For the first time, I asked him how his week went. Not much better than the weekend it seemed. He had no training for anything, no classes to go to and no job. It was a case of filling in time it seemed – a lot of time.

"There's TV," I suggested.

"I watch a lot of that," he admitted. "I've never been a reader so I don't get a newspaper. The lady in the Library cuts the crosswords out for me and I do them. There are a couple of billiard tables when we get Association but it can be hard getting on to them. Everyone has the same idea. I spend time cleaning my cell but that doesn't take long. I sleep a bit during the day but not too much, in case I can't sleep at night. It's the weekend that's the killer."

He was at the beginning of his sentence so, hopefully, things would change for him. A job might turn up or, better still, something in education which would occupy him.

He perked up a bit but it was a dismal visit. 'If you can't do the time…' had a different meaning for me after that.

Chapter 15

Some men serving long sentences find making conversation, even small talk, hard. Each day inside is a re-run of the one before. The next day will be exactly the same. Conversation, such as it is, follows a pattern.

"So, how's it going?" I ask.

"You know, same old, same old."

"Been watching much TV?" And so on.

Thomas was different. For one thing, he was older than most inmates I saw, probably mid-forties. When I saw him first, he could not stop talking. When he sketched out what had happened, I could understand why. His story was that he had originally served a long term for rape. After being out on licence for almost as long he was re-arrested. His account of how this came about spilled out of him in a rush. He would become emotional, stop for a while to compose himself and then pick up the thread again.

He went over the details, which were fairly sparse, each time I visited him. This is how it went.

"I had just come off nightshift and I decided to go to the park before going home. I sat in the car for a while then went to the Gents toilet. There was no one else around but when I came out, the park keeper had reported me to the police. They took me to the Station."

He elaborated on every detail of what happened. Then he went over it all again. I had the feeling he had gone over these details in his head time and time again. It was almost as though he was dictating the events in the park to himself and not to me.

Whichever it was, the words kept pouring out. He began to add details to it at each visit. He went on to tell me that he had been given a strict Catholic upbringing. This, he claimed, had affected his attitude to sex. He felt sure that this had contributed to his offence of rape. He had kept to the conditions of his licence until the incident in the park. What happened, or did not happen in the gents' toilet, had brought him back to prison. The incident was considered reminiscent of his rape offence. On those grounds, it was decided he could still be a danger to the public.

He was clearly terrified of what the outcome would be. If found guilty, he would be back inside to finish off his original sentence. Thus, the weekly pouring out of the details to me as though that might change things for him. For six visits, he never spoke of anything else as though he wanted to convince me of his innocence. He went over the same familiar ground every week. Sometimes, he elaborated a bit but basically, he kept to the same story. Occasionally, he referred to 'my offences' rather than 'my offence'. It was as though he could convince me he had done nothing wrong that would make a difference to what would happen to him. I found it very hard knowing what to say to him.

My experience of visiting Mark meant that we had mostly talked generalities. Unlike Thomas, after our first visit, Mark never referred to the offence which had brought him in to prison. With Thomas, we spoke of nothing else.

I began to dread the visits since it was impossible for me to convince him that things might be all right. Who knew, apart from Thomas, what the truth was. I just know he was absolutely desperate. I tried every now and then to switch the conversation round to anything else.

I was, occasionally, asked to do a few hours in the visits centre since they were short of volunteers. This just involved serving refreshments to the visitors waiting to go over to the visits hall. I tried explaining to Tom how the centre operated, how busy it got and how many children were part of it. I even started telling him what sort of things were sold at the tea bar. I wanted anything which would give us something else to talk about.

Since his parents visited him, he asked me to keep an eye open for them at my next stint in the centre. I thought that was a bit of a long shot but I said I would. As it happened, I did see them. They were easy to spot since they were so much older than the other visitors and stood apart from them. Also, they looked over to me at the tea bar so it was obvious that Tom had described me to them. I found it painfully difficult since for one thing, they looked tired and wretched. I worried they thought I was in some professional capacity in the prison and could be helpful to their son. Nothing could have been further from the truth. We exchanged a few words and that was it. When their visits number was called, they shook hands with me and thanked me for what I was doing for Thomas.

Suddenly, my visits to their son were over and he was released. His story had been believed. I was relieved for him. I was relieved for myself since I had felt so helpless. I was glad our visits had come to an end. I never wanted to see anyone else or those closest to them in such a wretched state again.

Chapter 15a

I learned that the pros and cons of having a single or a double cell was a tricky one. For Phil, the answer was definitely a single one. Sadly, when I met him, he had just been allocated a double. He looked decidedly gloomy.

"Be a bit of company," I suggested. "Especially when you're locked up so much. Gives you someone to talk to."

"That's the trouble," he told me.
"For one thing, they've put me in with a Geordie and I can't stand them. This one talks a load of rubbish. Can't make out half he says, anyway."

I toyed with suggesting that this might be a good thing but decided against it. Phil didn't look in the mood to be cheered up.

"You could ask to get on another wing. Might get a single there."

"Not much chance. Most want a single."

Poor Phil. I felt for him. Being thrown together with an inmate you couldn't get on with would be hard. Fortunately, his sentence was short which solved his problem.

I learned from another inmate how this business of singles or doubles can be made easier. "You look around at Association and weigh up who you would share with," he said.

"How would that work?" I asked.

"Well, you don't want someone who mouths off all the time. Ones who throw their weight around. Think they're the big cheese. Then there's where they come from. I mean, their accents. For me, I'd avoid a Scot, especially a Glaswegian. I shared with one once. Aggressive little bugger he was. Five foot nothing. No, not a Scot."

"I can see that," I said.

I reckoned he was one of the few of my visits who hadn't picked up on my accent.

Chapter 16

I learned, by trial and error, how to approach the question of a prisoner's offence. Sometimes, a prisoner will say at the start of visits why he is inside. It's as though he wants to set the record straight right away. Others build up to it and then drop it casually into the conversation. After that, they don't make any further reference to it. It doesn't affect the visitor either way since it's not part of visiting. The more visits I did, the more relaxed they became. Apart from the visits which, for one reason or another, I knew were going to be difficult, they all seemed perfectly natural and easy since they were mostly just small talk.

Dave never revealed what his offence was but after a couple of visits, I made an inspired guess only to myself, why he was inside. The longer the visits went on, the more sure I became that I was right. I knew he wouldn't tell me. Somehow, that made me even more sure.

There was something about the over-familiar way he had of talking to me right from the start. It was as though we were old mates so we could be frank with each other. He started off on a religious bent which was unusual. Few prisoners, in my experience, mention their religious beliefs. I certainly never mentioned mine. Dave wanted to establish his right away.

"With me," he said. "I'm not really religious in a conventional way but I suppose you could say I was a spiritual kind of guy. And I know there is someone up there. You know what I mean, don't you? It's a big part of my life, all our lives I suppose Affects the way you live, doesn't it."

It occurred to me that it hadn't had much of an effect on him since he was doing a long stretch. The more he embellished on this account of his spiritual side, the less convinced I was. The more he worked on his technique, the more convinced I was of his offence.

He noted the crucifix round my neck and nodded approvingly.

"We all need someone to see us through, don't we?"

I avoided reacting to this and gradually, he changed tack. After that, he began to tell me in some detail about the relationship he had with his girlfriend.

"We all need that closeness, that togetherness with someone, don't we? I expect that's been your experience as well. You must feel that."

I guessed this was more than the spiritual togetherness of the previous weeks.

This line of talk developed as the visits continued.

"The feeling of that closeness, of touching someone. You must know what I mean," he persisted.

Once he was on this topic, he never lost eye contact with me. He looked a bit misty eyed and moved nearer me, as far as the bolted down chair would allow.

Fraud, I told myself, *definitely fraud.* I was right, as I discovered. It wasn't too hard. He had seen me as a gullible woman he could soften up a bit with the right kind of patter. First spirituality and then sex.

I was relieved when he was released, 'shipped out' in prison jargon. Not because of his offence. I just reckoned I had exhausted my variety of nods and non-committal responses.

Chapter 17

If anyone asks me about prison and prison visiting, they are sure to put this question. If it's so bad, why do they keep going back in there? One of the explanations is that many of them simply have nowhere to go when they are released.

When I started going into prison, I had the naïve idea that once given a release date, the inmate I was visiting would be delighted. Not so. Their first thought was where they were going to stay. Since so many of them came from broken homes, they weren't going back to the bosom of the family. The best they could hope for was getting bed space in a friend's flat. That never sounded fool proof to me. Even if their sentence has been short, the ties they had with the outside are more likely to be broken.

"I've left my stuff at my mate's so I should be ok there. Even a night or two would be a start," they would tell me.

There's sometimes a suggestion their mum would take them back, depending on her new boyfriend. There's an ex-girlfriend who might if she hadn't met someone else… Clutching at straws is as good as it gets for some.

There's hostel accommodation if that's available but for those who have experience of it, that's not an option. It's easy to get drugs and hard to hold on to what possessions you have are only two of the problems there. Some hostels mean you have to be out during the day with all the temptation that has for an ex-prisoner.

For many, getting a release date is tempered with 'where am I going to stay'…

Chapter 18

Some of the men I visit drop the odd swear word in conversation generally followed with a polite 'oh, sorry, miss'. Geoff's conversation was different. His talk was peppered with a variety of swear words. It had obviously become such a habit, he couldn't stop it. I couldn't be offended since it was part of his normal conversation and I couldn't do much about it unless I stopped visiting him. At first, I would raise an eyebrow or assume a pained expression but apart from the obligatory, 'oh, sorry, miss', it didn't stop him. He was like someone with an unusual speech defect and I don't suppose he was even aware of it.

The thing is there was something very likeable about him. He had the air of an innocent which sat oddly with his choice of language. I once stopped him in mid-flow and asked,
"What would you think if I talked to you like that, Geoff?"

He looked puzzled.

"Like what, miss?"

"Swearing."

"Don't know. I don't mind, miss."

"Oh well, never mind, Geoff. Go on with what you were saying anyway."

I gave the eyebrow raising and the pained expression a rest after that. I know when I'm beaten.

Chapter 19

My first visit, which was to Mark, lasted about eight months. Others were much shorter, sometimes only two or three weeks and then the inmate was abruptly transferred to another institution. I was glad my visiting started off in that way. It didn't occur to me when I began visiting that the length of time I knew an inmate would make such a difference to me. Seeing someone only two or three times, gave little chance of getting to know them. There were different reasons for that since they could have been transferred elsewhere, couldn't be bothered to come over (something better on TV) or had been released. The latter was good news for them but the following week, I had to make some connection with a new face and name. Visitors never got any warning that their visit was cancelled until they arrived there. When that happens one week, you are likely to be seeing a new face the following one.

Visiting the same person for months rather than weeks made more sense to me and, I think, would be more helpful to the inmate. They are more relaxed and outgoing as the weeks go by, and I see changes in them the more time we have together. For me, these kind of visits become more rewarding. When I first visited Alan, his problem with his teenage son was on his mind. It had been poor before he came into prison and difficult to repair now he was inside. He found it hard to build bridges between them when they were dependent on telephone calls. These didn't help at first and then over a few weeks, I could sense that things were improving.

I could see Mark, the first person I visited, change from a very nervous youngster experiencing his first time in prison, to someone optimistic about starting again on the outside. With Thomas, terrified, he could be facing another long term inside, I could see that he needed time to go over and over the details of his offence. Seeing him only once or twice wouldn't have helped nor would a change of visitor. He needed some sense of continuity if it was only a chance to repeat the same phrases over and over.

All three men would face different problems on the outside. Mark had no settled plans, for jobs, money or accommodation on release. Alan couldn't be sure that a few phone calls from prison would really solve the breach between him and his son. Thomas because of the seriousness of his offence had more problems. Still, all three had been given another start and were hopeful. I wanted to be hopeful for them.

Chapter 20

E wing in the prison held not only sex offenders, but other inmates described as 'vulnerable'. I learned that these could be prison officers, police, or legals. These are inmates who could choose to be on E wing since for different reasons, life might be made difficult for them on other wings.

Soon after visiting Thomas, I was given an E wing prisoner to visit, a sex offender called Jake. I could see then how Thomas felt not only about returning to prison but as a sex offender. No matter what their specific offence was, in prison parlance, they were referred to as 'nonces' – the bottom of the heap.

In the visits hall, they are sitting separately from other prisoners. For this visit, I was directed to a table where other E wing men were being visited. Although I was aware of this 'separate' existence for sex offenders, it still felt odd. It was even odder hearing Mass in the prison Chapel where I could see the E wing men sitting in pews separated from the rest. They weren't allowed to join the evening Bible class in the Chapel. Apparently, this was considered a security problem. The mix of 'ordinary' prisoners and sex offenders was always thought of as dangerous. I didn't get to know Jake, or what his specific offence was, since he was moved out just after our visits started. He was very quiet on that one visit and he found conversation difficult.

Although I didn't have time to find out how life was like for him, it was an eye opener for me. It kept reminding me of Thomas and his fear of being sent back in to serve the rest of his sentence. No wonder he was terrified.

A visitor could say 'no' to visiting a sex offender if they felt strongly enough about it. Personally, I found that strange but another visitor gave me a different slant on that.

One of our visitors, Jonathan, was a committed Christian and a regular churchgoer. He was a bit strait laced but committed to visiting which he had been doing for years. He told me he had made it clear from the start that although he loved visiting, he couldn't visit a sex offender. A point came when there was only one prisoner who had asked for a visit and, yes, he was a sex offender. Reluctantly, Jonathan said he would do it. This was a time when visits were allowed in cells rather than the hall.

"I don't quite know how it happened," he told me. THEIR visits had continued for some time and I think Jonathan was still puzzled by that.

"We just got on from the first visit. There was no problem at all," he told me. Don't ask me how it worked out like that.

He told me that none of his friends at Church were interested in his prison visiting. They had never once made a reference to it. They seemed to be disappointed at what he was doing so he soon stopped bringing the subject up.

I know they would have been shocked at me visiting a sex offender but the two of us seemed to get on from the start. We talked a lot and I looked forward to our visits.

Apparently, Jonathan's inmate, Pete, was a big Cliff Richards fan.

At one visit, this fellow was desperately trying to remember one of Cliff's hits. Just recalling it brought a smile to Jonathan's face.

"I laughed afterwards to think how friends would have felt seeing the two of us," Jonathan told me.

"There was some song this chap was trying to remember. I was no help but he kept insisting I would know it."

He kept saying it's that one, you know. It goes, sort of, and then he'd hum it a bit. I tried doing the same thing but kept getting it wrong. No, no, he'd say it's more like and he'd hum another bit. There were the two of us singing some mixed up Cliff Richards hits together. It must have taken up half of the visit.

I liked the idea of Jonathan singing along with Cliff, even if he didn't recognise the songs. Jonathan had to give up visiting, eventually, due to ill health. That was a loss for both of them. Pete lost a good visitor in Jonathan. I don't know if he ever got another visitor but if he did, I hope he was a Cliff Richards fan.

Chapter 21

Most of the men I visited had some history of drug taking. Committing a crime to pay for their habit was what brought them into prison in the first place. One of the saddest comments I heard on drug taking inside was from a Governor who told me,

"They come in here drug free but develop a drug habit once they are in here."

Being in prison didn't stop them using since drugs were routinely smuggled in. It meant taking a chance on the random searches which were done frequently but for most of them, that seemed a risk worth taking. Sometimes, it was for personal use, sometimes, it was used as barter, trading it to another prisoner. While users might manage to stay off drugs inside, their problem came up when they were released. A common story was that an old friend would give you a small amount for free, then, of course, you were hooked. Back to the old spiral of stealing to pay for your habit and ending up back inside. It was a pathetic story but one I heard a lot.

I was given an object lesson on how it worked from the business end of things when I spent some time with Gordy. I wasn't his visitor. This was just a chance encounter when I was waiting to sort out my next visit. Dealing drugs was his business and a very lucrative business, it seemed to me. It was also run on very business-like lines. Mobile phones and a selection of different numbers, figured prominently. He told me what the rewards were for him, a nice flat and expensive cars. "I love cars," he said. He only wanted to talk about his 'business'. I expect he thought I would be impressed.

He was well over 6 ft. and massively built. His Afro hair-do added another couple of inches to his height. He was a fearsome looking figure. I presume that stood him well in his line of work. He told me how dealing worked in such a matter of fact manner, he made it sound like a legitimate business. He boasted about his success with women, many of whom, he assured me, would be waiting for him on release.

It was obvious why he did it since the rewards, for him, seemed huge.

It was a daft question but I couldn't resist asking him.

He didn't want to hear anything from me but I couldn't let it pass.

"You are selling stuff which kills people. Is it never on your conscience? I mean, doesn't that ever bother you?"

He wasn't offended by the question. He had probably been asked it before. He just smiled and said,
"Well, if I wasn't selling it, they would get it from someone else. Might as well be me."

Under different circumstances, I would have found his size and appearance intimidating. It was no doubt useful in his line of business as well as in a prison situation. His reputation inside appeared to be well established. A prisoner who knew I had been Gordy's captive audience gave me a word of caution.

"If you ever see Gordy on the out, miss, just give him a quick wave and cross the road."

Chapter 22

Once a prisoner is released then all contact with him comes to an end. Your visiting could have been long or short but once he is out that gate, that's it. There's the possibility of seeing him by chance, but that's different. The unwritten rule, if that happens, is never to give him money since in most cases, it's obvious where the money will go. A cheery greeting and buying him a coffee is all that's acceptable. One visitor told me of seeing someone she had visited in the city centre near where she lived. He was obviously sleeping rough. She bought him coffee and a sandwich.

"Breakfast in bed," she joked.

It's not always as comfortable or as easy as that. Jake's face was familiar to me although I had never visited him. Once I started Chaplaincy visiting, I saw some of the men who came over to the Chapel for the Bible group so he was probably one of them. Walking round the local market one Saturday morning, I saw a vaguely familiar face. It took a few seconds to work out where I knew him from. Whether he had seen me first, I don't know but he moved away quickly. It was Jake. I caught up with him but he looked embarrassed. I think he would rather I had just passed on. He said he was fine. He looked far from fine. After a few awkward moments, he moved off quickly and the moment had gone.

His was just one of the familiar faces from the Bible group but I couldn't say I knew him and he didn't know me. It's different when it's someone you have visited over a long period. If the visits have gone well, a kind of fellow feeling develops. Trying to explain this to a friend, I said,

"You learn things about them even on a short visit. They confide in you since they have nothing to fear from that. They cannot be like that with an officer or a fellow prisoner. You get to like them."

My friend's expression said it all. "You mean you <u>like</u> these people?" End of conversation.

Another friend made clear her attitude to offenders in much the same way. We were shopping together one afternoon when I spotted a familiar face. I mumbled a quick explanation to her and went over just to say 'hello, how's it going'. My friend shot quickly out of sight.

"I'll wait for you across the road," she said.

Visiting Carl was hard going. It was harder than usual to make any contact with him. From the word go, he looked so downcast and had nothing to say. After a few weeks, he gradually lightened up and trotted out his pet phrase.

"I'm getting there, though. I'm getting there."

At his last visit, he threw his arms round me. I had never seen him so animated.

"I'm getting out on the tag," he said.

He was one of the people I bumped into on his release. He saw me first and greeted me like a long lost relative. I don't know what passers-by would have thought since he pulled up the leg of his jeans, pointing to the tag and said with a laugh, "My fashion accessory, miss."

Chapter 23

Most men worry as their release date gets nearer. That seemed like a contradiction to me at first. Later, it made sense. Their problems were put on hold while they were inside but once released, they were faced with so many. Unless they were lucky, they had no money, no job and nowhere to stay. That was the usual story. Also, of course, they had a prison record. Not one to inspire confidence once you are walking out of the prison gates. The money they are given, about £46, can disappear quickly. Gerry was more worried than most, although he tried to hide it or at least put a gloss on it.

Our opening conversation was the same every week, apart from the number of days he had left. Like most inmates, he always counted in days rather than weeks or months.

"Its 19 days now," he told me.
"Doesn't seem long so I am trying not to think about it. Well, I do think about it, but I'm trying not to think about it."

To me, the way he put it, sounded comical but to him it made perfect sense.

Gerry told me he had been living with a mate although I felt it was a pretty casual arrangement. He expected to move back in with this mate when he was released.

"I've phoned him a few times but it didn't work," he told me. "Must have changed his mobile. Yes, that could be it."

He didn't have a job to go to. I'd never visited a prisoner who had. But that wasn't his main worry. All his possessions were in his mate's flat. Not only that,

"He's been looking after my money for me. That's with my stuff. That'll be all alright, I know. I've known him for a while. I knew he wouldn't visit but I thought he might write. Yes, I reckon he must have changed his mobile."

That seemed a good moment to change that line of talk.

"Do you have much in here to take out with you?" I asked him.

"Not much. All my stuff is in my mate's flat, jeans, trainers, everything. And the money. Last time I got out, he'd been wearing some of my tee shirts. That was ok. I didn't mind that. The money should be all right though."

It didn't look promising. I think that was beginning to dawn on Gerry as well.

Hoping to change the subject, I said,
"Hope they don't give you one of those HMP bags when you leave."

"Don't think so. Last place I was in, they gave you a plain black sack. Waiting at the station, you could see other guys with them. Everyone in the town knew where you'd come from. Didn't need to have HMP on it."

Gerry was vague about his family who hadn't visited or written. There was an even vaguer mention of a girlfriend and the hope she might meet him at the gate on release. No family support, a vanishing mate and, possibly, a girlfriend. It didn't look like much of a safety net.

He had learned something about cooking while inside. I reminded him of the recipes we'd discussed. Shepherd's pie and apple crumble were his favourites. He never mentioned any others so I reckon these were the only two he had mastered.

"I'll be doing them when I'm out. No more take-away for me. I'll go to the supermarket, buy the ingredients and do my own cooking."

That was something, I suppose. Quite where he would be putting his newfound skill into practice was a bit vague. My next visit was a wasted one since he had already been shipped out. I hoped at least some of his plans worked out for him. As with all of my visits, I would never know.

Chapter 24

Alistair was starting to look more upbeat when he came over for his visits which was a relief. He was very quiet and having no visits from friends or family, he had little to say about anything. As with some inmates, having a prison visitor just meant a chance to get away from the wing. That's how it was for Alistair. For some reason, I started our hour with a breezy 'so what's new'. He looked a bit sheepish and said,

"I got a letter today."

"You look pleased. From your girlfriend?"

"I'm not sure, miss. I mean she might be." And then, he told me the story.

His cellmate did have a regular visitor, his sister and on one occasion, she brought her friend along, mostly I think to share the driving. What came out of this sounded something like prison dating to me. Alistair's cellmate, Jamie, told him about the girl. The sister told her girlfriend about Alistair and one thing lead to another. They wrote to each other and that was it.

"She's going to visit. I've sent her the V.O."

It was hard to know how to react but he looked so pleased about this I didn't want to put a dampener on it.

"I don't suppose you know much about her, just from a letter, I mean."

"She's going to send me a picture next time she writes. Then it'll be a visit. I can't wait."

I told him that was great. It was hard to say anything else since he looked so pleased.

"You won't know much about each other. You could write regularly and learn more."

"No, a visit would be better. I'm no good at letters. That one was hard enough. Jamie helped me with it."

"How old is Jamie?"

"Oh, I don't know but he made a good job of the letter. He said to put love, Alistair, at the end."

"Good idea."

I wasn't sure that any of this was a good idea. It was a novel way of meeting someone but if it helped him get through his sentence, that was something. I just hoped nobody would get hurt along the way.

Chapter 25

One of the thing I sensed from inmates, especially those facing a long sentence, is their fear of being forgotten on the outside, of losing touch. When they spoke of best mates or family members who always 'loved them to bits', I could sense some wishful thinking. I suppose the most tenuous connection with someone on the outside was better than nothing. I thought Alistair's idea that something could transpire from a girl he knew nothing about was a one off. I presumed his optimistic attitude was down to something a teenager would come up with... Not so, according to a fellow visitor. She knew of similar stories and they weren't all youngsters.

As is the way with visiting, I never learned how Alistair's story worked out. I hoped he, or the girl, wasn't expecting too much from it. He had no link with anyone on the outside and this must have looked like some kind of lifeline. Family relationships can break down easily especially for someone with a long sentence. Home and prison can be miles apart, and that doesn't help. Friends who might keep in touch eventually break off. When that lifeline stops, life goes bleaker for the inmate.

Alistair might have been clutching at straws but that's understandable. Even inmates who still have some home ties fret that things can go wrong. Letters or phone calls are not much of a substitute and wrong messages can be picked up from them. Few of the men I met had much in the way of communication skills which doesn't help.

I did feel dubious when Alistair told me about the letter but however it worked out, it was at least breaking the tedium of his sentence if only for a while. When I later heard of older inmates making that kind of connection on the word of a fellow cellmate, I wasn't so sure. One example from my fellow visitor was one involving a woman with a child at home. What the expectations were on both sides, I don't know but it seemed fraught with more difficulties than Alistair's idea. Who knows…

Chapter 26

This was an occasion when I sat in the visits hall for longer than usual waiting for Geoff. Not everything falls into place for a visit so I wasn't concerned. Things can go wrong with visits as I learned. They did more than once for me, whether I was waiting in the hall or the Chaplaincy and that's just accepted. Spending time studying both inmates and their visitors in the hall is not the done thing. A cursory glance is enough, or maybe a nod and a smile at a familiar face. This particular day, out of the blue, something struck me while I waited. It was the same familiar scene, an inmate on one side of the table, his visitors at the other and children wandering around. In other words, nothing new there except I thought for the first time – how come people accept this? This is not the way things are meant to be.

Maybe it's because I had seen both sides of prison, the inmates I visited and the people I had seen in the visits centre preparing to come over. From the men, I heard their gripes about prison life and what it would be like when they were released. From the people I saw in the visits centre, I knew little except what I observed before they went over and when they came back. I had seen visitors and visited sitting together many times without giving much thought to it. There was nothing different about it that day, so why I had that light bulb moment I don't know. It was probably down to the long wait I was having but it felt profound at the time.

I was brought down to earth with a cheery,

"Sorry about the wait, miss. Usual cock-up with that lot over there. What can you do, eh?"

Well, I suppose this was some kind of reality, for Geoff anyway.

Chapter 27

You can't argue with the rules, whether you are an inmate or a visitor. I still think you can question them or at least ask for an explanation since they are often arbitrary. Things I did early on in my visiting were acceptable and now I was told they were not. I decided to raise this point at one of our monthly meetings where one of the Governors was invited as a guest speaker. The idea was that he would address any of the problems we had with our visits. I told him that more than once, I had given something to an inmate I was visiting. Why not now, I wanted to know.

"No, I don't think that could have happened. You wouldn't have been allowed."

I could only mutter under my breath, "Oh, yes I did," but clearly he wasn't listening.

At the same meeting, since the business of rules was being discussed, another visitor questioned why he hadn't been allowed to give a good luck card as a memento to an inmate due for release.

"That may have happened at one time, but not now," he was told. "It was against the rules."

When it was coming up to Christmas, one of our new visitors handed a £5 note to the inmate she was visiting. He explained it to an officer, thinking this might be the right thing to do. It might have been for him but not the visitor who received notification from the prison that her visiting was now over.

When the Sikh chaplain brought in sweetmeats for his group one evening, the officer in charge shook his head. "Not allowed," he said. The chaplain stood his ground saying this had been allowed before. His wife had made them specially for the men and he didn't intend taking them back home again.

He had successfully brought them up to the Chaplaincy once when I was visiting, so I knew they were mouth-watering. Anyway, phone calls were made, one word led to another and eventually, he and his sweetmeats triumphed. A small victory for both Chaplain and his sweetmeats.

Chapter 28

At one of my first visits, I arrived at the same time as a prison van with its small blacked out windows dropping off new inmates. Later, I saw the new arrivals being escorted to where they would be processed through the system, carrying their black bags of property. It's not a cheering sight. That's the first night of their sentences. It made me wonder how much stuff they would need to see them through their time inside. It was Neil, a talkative Yorkshire lad, who put me straight on that.

"I came straight from Court so I didn't have much. I remember I didn't have a toothbrush with me. That was my first mistake…The one they give you in here isn't worth a toss. The toothpaste is about the same. I used that for putting up posters in my cell.

You're given bedding and stuff, plastic cutlery, a bowl and a plate. There's also a bar of soap, toothpaste, shaving soap and two razors. They're all cheap crap but they start you off. That's your entitlement each month although it doesn't always work out like that.

If you're lucky and have a decent cellmate, that can help. I've known lads in my last place who've passed on toiletries, sometimes a pair of old trainers which is useful. Toiletries is the big thing. You don't want to be sharing with someone who is short of decent soap and deodorant. I've been lucky with cellmates – so far."

I learned from another inmate that a standard prisoner, one who has just come in, gets £15.50 of his own money to spend as well as what he earns in prison. An enhanced inmate gets more. A good job, say working in the laundry or the kitchen, pays more than sweeping the wings.

After that, your hope is in having a good cellmate and, more importantly, the support of friends and family on the outside.

Chapter 29

Sometimes talk flows during a visit and it's a surprise when 'time's up' is called. Mostly, it's a stop—start conversation but that works as well.

With Nick, it was neither. He had nothing to say at all. Literally, nothing. That was alarming when I started to visit. For one thing, it was hard to work out why he had asked for a visit in the first place. I did ask him at one point why he had asked for a visitor but he seemed to take offence at that so I didn't pursue it. A crowded visits hall was a change from his single cell so I suppose that was enough for him.

He had been inside for a long time since his sentence was 'indeterminate'. That system has been stopped but for Nick, it meant he had no idea when he would be released.

He did endless courses which were meant to help prepare him for release whenever that might be. Anger Management, Drugs Awareness, AA meetings and more. If the prison didn't cater for a particular course, he could be transferred to an establishment which did. He told me the names of the different prisons he had passed through. He seemed a classic case of someone who was institutionalised. I would ask him about the course he was on or what it was happening on his wing. Whatever it was I tried to dredge up, his response was minimal. There were times when I dreaded going in and thought the visiting hour would never end.

He had one visit which was from his sister. When he told me that was in the pipeline, I thought 'great'. At our next visit, I pounced on that asking what she had said, how she was, did it go well, did her partner come as well, etc. There was the customary shrug.

"There was nothing to talk about," he said.

His only topic was what he watched on TV. That was mostly the soaps. Once he got on to that, he would recount the plots to me in detail. For some reason, he thought I was a fan. I started watching the occasional one to see if I could offer anything but his knowledge was encyclopaedic, my meagre input didn't match up. He spoke about the plots and the characters involved as though this was real life. He tried to work out what would happen in the next episodes, even asking my slant on that. Maybe they were the closest to real life he ever got. It was as though he really knew these soap characters.

When he did get on to something, it was always to do with TV, he wouldn't let go and spoke in a circular kind of way about it. I tried putting in a comment every now and then but he didn't want to be interrupted. It was a very one-sided conversation.

I did discover, however, that he felt strongly about what was right and what was wrong. The topic was so unlikely that I couldn't see it making sense and anyway once he started, he didn't want to be interrupted. I had mentioned something about my car journey to the prison and filling up with petrol before I started up.

"You get paid for that," he said.

"No, I don't claim expenses," I told him. "I could but I have never got round to it. Doesn't amount to much anyway. I know you'd have to fill up so many forms. I'm not very good at forms."

It was unusual for him to ask me a direct question so I was pleased. I reckoned that form filling as a subject was as good as any.

That started him off. He was like a terrier with a bone. He wouldn't let the subject drop.

"Shouldn't be allowed," he said. "They should pay you." He went on about this until I thought, for once, he would never stop talking. I put in the occasional, 'no, I'm really not bothered' but he wouldn't be dissuaded. I couldn't believe anyone could talk at such length and with such feeling about something so insignificant. He was like someone incensed by a grave injustice. I tried changing the subject but he wouldn't have it.

Eventually, he started to wind down but it was an eye opener for me. Why would he care about something that didn't affect him and at such length when he had nothing to say about a visit from his sister. I couldn't work it out. I was sure he would bring it up the following week but oddly enough, he never referred to it again. For our next visit, we were back to the soaps.

Chapter 30

Telling anyone I go into prison every week, continued to be a conversation stopper. I've brought it up in company and had no response whatsoever. I mean, there was complete silence. It was as though mentioning it was a social faux pas. Maybe people feel there is something suspect about my doing it. Maybe they disapprove but feel too embarrassed to say anything. Maybe it's because it doesn't impinge on their lives. They're thinking, perhaps, she's one of these muddle headed do-gooders. Let's not encourage her. I could probably come up with some more 'maybes' but I've never come up with a suitable explanation.

I've had hostile reactions. They tell me that these people have committed a crime as though I didn't know that. That's why they are in there, they remind me, so leave them to it. For some reason, they always sound indignant. I suppose some of it is down to misinformation. Their idea of prison life has come from films, TV or the more lurid tabloid tales of how cushy it is inside. Much of this is taken as gospel. At least, it's a reaction which is better than nothing at all. Nothing at all is mostly what I get.

Occasionally, one of the men I visit asks why I do it. Do I get paid for it? Am I a social worker? No to both questions. Some of them are quite puzzled as to why I would want to do it. "Why do you want to come in here, miss," they ask. The thing is I don't know myself except that I find it rewarding as well as enjoyable. Truth is, I was pressured into it by another prison visitor. I agreed to it since I couldn't think of a polite way to refuse. Nevertheless, I knew from my first visit, this was something I really wanted to do and hoped I could go on doing it. Simple as that.

I was once told by a charity worker that this was one thing she could never do.

"I'd have nothing in common with these people," she explained to me. "I mean what could I say to them."

Maybe there's a clue in that. Maybe I do it because their lives have little in common with mine or that of my friends and family. It's definitely not a case of 'there but for the grace of God go I' but, thinking about it there is this. Prison visiting has affected me in one way or another, although, I can't quite put my finger on what. That seems as good a reason as any to keep doing it.

Chapter 31

Visitors arrive first at the visits centre. They show staff their V.O.s and have their ID checked. They stow their belonging into a locker and buy some refreshments while they wait for the number of their visit to be called out. All they can take to the hall is some cash for refreshments there and their V.O.

The centre was my first experience of the prison. Working at the tea bar meant I could, occasionally, had a word with visitors. If there was any mistake with ID, their visit couldn't take place. First, disbelief and then, tears were shed. Some of them came long distance by public transport. They either didn't realise it had to be picture ID or that they needed separate ID for each person with them including a baby. There were grandmothers, mothers and young girlfriends, some with a baby in arms.

Gradually, the packed centre emptied and volunteers did some clearing up until the first lot of visitors came back. Tears again for some because of 'a bad visit'. The occasional 'never again. That's my last time here'. But familiar faces kept returning for repeat visits.

I found the gap between the centre being emptied and visitors coming back to collect their belongings tedious. Being a volunteer rather than staff, I had no role except selling the crisps and drinks. There might be one or two who don't go over for the visit and wait behind in the centre. I had nowhere to sit so standing behind the coffee bar was hard on my feet and my back. Then I would long for a customer to come over and break the monotony. I did until one week, a man came over to me. Maybe like me, he was bored waiting for the visitors to come back. He certainly looked disgruntled.

He didn't buy anything, just said,

"Well, you're not exactly rushed off your feet, are you?"

He went back to his seat and I went back to leaning on the counter.

Chapter 32

It's hard to say where conversation comes from on a visit. One of my visits to Hugh centred almost entirely on food. That was surprising since Hugh was built like a whippet and always came to his visit at high speed, with an odd springy kind of step. Like most prisoners, he complained about the food – "stodgy and soggy mashed potatoes" being top of his list, but on this occasion, he said,

"One of the first thing I'm going to eat when I get out is marmalade. I'm going to have marmalade on my toast."

"No chance of getting that in here. I love it."

"No, I could never eat that," I told him. "Jam, yes, honey maybe, but definitely not marmalade. Those stringy bits of peel would put me off."

"You're kidding," he said.

"No, seriously. I don't even like the look of it. I'll tell you what I used to love. Haven't had it for ages. Corn beef on a sandwich."

Hugh looked horrified.

"You're kidding. You eat corn beef?"

"Seriously, its lovely and it makes a great sandwich. If you put tomato with it, that's even better. It has to be on brown bread, of course. I never eat white."

Hugh was still mulling over the idea of someone eating corn beef.

"One thing I could never eat is porridge," I told him. "Terrible, me being a Scot."

"You could put a lot of sugar on it," Hugh suggested.

"Not where I come from, you couldn't."

Suddenly, we were batting food likes and dislikes backwards and forwards. I don't think we agreed on one but it made the visit hour go very quickly.

I always asked about reading when on a visit since the prison had a library. Sometimes, when inmates said they did read, they were referring to one of the tabloids. Few of them read a book.

Hugh did and his favourite was science fiction. As with the food, I couldn't share his taste in that either.

"I don't understand the appeal. I feel the same about crime fiction."

"Well, that's usually rubbish," Hugh informed me.

He insisted I try science fiction mentioning one or two titles. He told me what his next one might be if the library had it. I knew they didn't have a great choice so I decided to buy it for him. When I mentioned it to the chaplain, he told me I couldn't do that. Sending a book to a prisoner was not allowed.

"But I've sent things in before," I told him, remembering Mark's trainers.

"That must have been some time ago. No, that's changed now. You couldn't send it direct to him anyway. It would have to be addressed here, opened and gone through by security. They have to look through it, page by page."

I could see from his expression that security would not spend time on that.

"Rules change," he said.

So I was left with a book I didn't want and Hugh missed out on. Our loss was the local charity shop's gain. It certainly didn't encourage me to read science fiction.

Chapter 33

Alan was the most organised prisoner I ever visited. He had everything cut and dried for his release. He had one of the better jobs in the prison so he was letting that cash mount up in his account. He also had one or two scams going with other inmates, he told me, which added to his savings. I thought it best not to ask what these were. Alan kept his head down, got on with the officers and never got into trouble. He was working his way towards getting to an open prison. Since he had a qualification for forklift driving, he had no qualms about getting a job on release.

"I go to the gym as often as I'm allowed," he told me. "I do press-ups in my cell every morning. I want to be fit when I get out."

Everything was carefully worked out by Alan except for one thing, his relationship with his son.

We were a few visits in before he even mentioned him and that was with a shrug.

"Teenagers," he told me. "What can you do with them, eh?"

He told me in detail about his plans on every visit and how they would work out. He also told me that when his marriage broke up, the son had gone to live with his mother. It was obvious there was friction but as Alan kept pointing out.

"Can't be helped. One of those things. I've tried phoning him but he cuts me off. He just doesn't want to know."

As the visits went on and he got nearer to his release date, he made more reference to his son. That generally ended with a shrug and

"But what can you do, eh?"

Then he went back to phoning his son. His calls didn't sound too successful.

As the visits went on, Alan spoke less about his plans and opened up more about his son.

"I've not been the best dad, I know that. When I left my wife and moved in with the girlfriend, my boy just didn't want to know. What could I do?"

He persisted with the phone calls but as far as I could make out, they mostly ended in an angry exchange between them.

I sympathised with him since phone calls are tricky in prison. Problems hard to resolve on the outside are impossible in a prison phone call. For one thing, there is no privacy and time is limited when other prisoners are waiting. It's hard for someone at home to understand that. Once the prisoner is back in his cell, that's it. No chance to go back and sort things out on a second call.

When Alan got word that he was accepted for an open prison, he immediately phoned his son. That seemed to work well and I could see how relieved he was. That didn't last long since the date for him to be shipped out changed and kept changing. That was out of his control but hard for someone on the outside to understand that. I was never sure when I went in to see him whether it would be a wasted visit and he would be gone. After that, the son didn't believe he was getting out. It was out of Alan's hands, everything in prison is, but his son couldn't accept that

"I've told him when I'm at the open, I'll be eligible for a town visit and we could meet up," he said.

That had sounded good to the son at first but when Alan tried explaining that he didn't have an actual date, his son thought it was another ploy.

"He thinks I'm jerking him around," Alan told me.
"Can't blame him. I've let him down so many times in the past. I'm trying to tell him things are different now. I'm trying to make things right with him. Trouble, is he's heard all that in the past."

My next visit to Alan was a non-visit. He had been transferred to an open the previous day. I had no way of knowing if things worked out between Alan and his son or if, as looked more likely, it was too late for that.

Chapter 34

I already knew something about Dev before I met him which was unusual. This was a guarded comment from one of the chaplains along the lines of – he's had a terrible life. Another visitor who had met him briefly advised me.

"Maybe best not to ask anything. He won't open up to you anyway. He'll only tell you what he wants to. He likes to keep everything on the surface."

I didn't want or need to know his background anyway since that was not a part of prison visiting so that didn't bother me. This was the first time I had been given any details about a prisoner before meeting him. I was told that he had received some counselling while inside. Whether that had been of help to him, I didn't know and unless he made any reference to it, I didn't think I could bring it up. None of this prepared me for Dev. He spoke well and was very affable when we met. He obviously enjoyed talking, always a good thing so I felt we'd get on well. Although he was well over 6 ft. and built in proportion, there was something very gentle about him. He never sounded depressed or seemed as though he had any particular problem with prison. This was not what I expected. None of this suggested someone with a terrible past.

The visits got better every week. He obviously looked forward to them, giving me a crushing handshake when he arrived and when he left.

Talk was pretty general at first but it never flagged. Gradually, he brought in comments about his life on the outside. There had been a girlfriend, but –

"I rang her on her birthday once, but she hung up on me. She'd know I was inside."

He came from a large family, sisters and brothers, and countless nieces and nephews.

"They love me to bits," he told me. He smiled at the thought.

None of them had ever visited him since, as he explained, "They live too far away. This place is in the wilds."

He had a good sense of fun and always made me laugh. When I visited him one week, he told me he had been watching the film The Killing Fields with his cellmate. Although I had already seen it, he insisted on launching into details of it.

"The Vietcong killed the intellectuals first," he explained.

He looked at me seriously for a moment or two dwelling on that point.

"I'd have been all right. You'd have been mincemeat."

He had been in and out of prison more than half of his life. More in than out, as he put it.

Maybe I looked surprised or alarmed so he assured me, "Nothing violent. I've never used violence. It was all just stupid stuff. Burglary, mostly."

I guess he wasn't much of a burglar since, as he told me, he had been caught countless times.

Some prisoners like to explain away their crimes or tone them down a bit, but Dev's attitude was different. Crime was all he had ever known. It was what he did. He just wasn't any good at it.

His first offence was at age 11.

"They sent me to a young offenders place. It was some kind of a home. It wasn't too bad. I've been in a few of them. I didn't realise I would go there straight from court though. My mum was in court when they took me away… She went out of one door and I went out the other."

Each week, a few other details came out.

His life had been a succession of Children's Homes, foster parents and prisons. – some good, some bad. He admitted that he had run away from both Homes and different sets of foster parents.

Although he spoke about his family regularly, the details were vague. They never visited or wrote to him. The main thing as far as he was concerned was that – yes, they all loved him to bits.

Most of his sentences were short from three months to 18 months. He had been in a variety of prisons up and down the country.

"There's a guy on my wing I knew well from my last place. A lovely lad, we get on well. I was glad to see him."

"Must be strange when you meet someone you know."

"Oh, no. I nearly always meet someone I've been with before," he told me,

"I know one of the officers in here. I met him when I was in a prison up North. Knows me well. Always calls me by my first name. He's always been very fair with me."

He never once looked unhappy or complained about conditions inside.

The only time he got close to what his childhood had been like was to shake his head and say,

"It was mostly bad stuff. You know, bad stuff when I was young."

He never elaborated on what the bad stuff was. He had obviously buried it away. Whether that worked for him or not, I never knew. I guessed he was about 40 years old and by his estimate he had spent more than half of that time in prison.

Chapter 35

So why do I visit and why do people think I visit? When I started ten years ago, I just knew this was for me. That's why I kept doing it but people want to look for different reasons.

They want to see me as a do-gooder. I've been told more than once,

"You're so good to be doing this."

Not so. Doing something you enjoy has nothing to do with goodness.

There's the implication, from some quarters, that I'll be judging the men I visit.

"Being judgmental is not part of the exercise, either."

But then, they insist,

"It gives you a chance to put them on the right path."

"There's the Justice system, the Probation, Social workers to handle that," I tell them.

It's hard to explain what motivates the prison visitor. Why would he, or she want to do it. Surely, they're a certain kind of person, as though they are all cut from the same pattern. It's easier to explain what they are not, rather than what they are. They are certainly not judgmental or they would not be doing it. A friend who had once toyed with the idea of visiting explained to me that he was attracted to the idea, but then drew back.

"If they could only keep their hands off other people's money and property," he said.

He sounded exasperated and I sort of knew what he meant. At least, he had put some thought to it. A bit kinder than 'they've broken the law. They're in there to be punished'.

Another friend, a woman, said she'd be nervous just going through the gate and frightened of speaking to a visitor. This was at a time when I still visited through the hall. I don't know what she would have made of one to one visiting in the Chaplaincy. I explained to her about the security in the prison and the presence of officers. I said I had never felt unsafe whether passing through the many gates or talking to a prisoner but I knew she would never be convinced. I could understand how she felt and sympathise with her but it didn't relate to my experience of visiting. The only unsettling incident I witnessed happened in the visits hall. That was frightening at the time but controlled by officers in minutes.

Maybe it was a lack of imagination on my part. I found few people were interested in visiting but only one, my sister, was baffled.

"If you saw a fight about to start in the town centre or a drunk anywhere near you, you'd cross the street to avoid it. How on earth are you doing this?"

She had a point but I couldn't explain at the time. I don't know if it would have helped but I could have repeated the old phrase – 'Because it's a different world in there.'

An Evangelical Christian, one of a group who met with the men regularly, assured me,
"You give these men such a good example – telling them about the Lord."

She looked disappointed when I explained that nothing was further from the truth. The prison visitee is not there to preach to prisoners. That's definitely not part of their remit. I wouldn't have been doing it if that was so. She was not convinced. She was still sure I should be showing them the error of their ways.

There's another faction who tell me – Surely I must feel nervous, mixing with 'these people'.

'These people', I try to explain seem just like people once you start visiting them.

It's been explained to me that I do it because I am naïve, something of an innocent. I'm like Pollyanna – always looking on the bright side, since I must think I'm making a difference. Once again, wrong.

I said yes to visiting because I couldn't think of a polite way to say no. Simple as that.

But these reactions are fine by me. At least, it gives me a chance to talk about prison visiting. What I don't understand is when it meets with complete indifference. That I do find hard.

Chapter 36

The first thing Darren noticed was the mirror. There was a decent sized mirror above the wash hand basin in this Chaplaincy room. He was delighted. According to him, the one in his cell was about the size of a postage stamp.

I was now able to visit through the Chaplaincy which meant I could see the prisoner on a one to one basis. That was a bonus for both inmate and visitor. Not having to go through security was another. For Darren, it was the mirror. He spent some time admiring himself from different angles, checking his hairstyle and smoothing down his tee shirt.

"Nice tee shirt," I told him. I wasn't sure whether the whole visit would be in front of this mirror.

"It's a designer," he told me.
"First time I've seen it properly."

He kept turning backwards and forwards to see if it looked as good at the back as at the front

Eventually, he chose one of the two swivel chairs and spent some time adjusting that before we began.

As an office, it didn't have much to recommend it – except, of course, for the mirror. That was quite small and hung low above the washbasin in an odd position. I had the feeling it was there to cover up a mark on the wall. The walls were prison beige, and apart from a computer and some files, that was all there was to it. There was a tiny fridge which Darren investigated and found it to be empty. There were bars on the window but, of course, no view of the outside world. We could see a patch of corridor and occasionally, an officer moving at some speed along it.

"Trouble," Darren assured me.

"When you see them running like that, they're usually running in the wrong direction away from trouble," he said.

As office space goes, it was completely anonymous. Maybe it wasn't used much but it pleased Darren. I suppose it was the touch of normality which appealed to him. It was far from cosy but it was a big improvement on the visits hall and of course, on his cell. Oddly enough, it wasn't much of a visit but just being in this different environment kept Darren entertained. At intervals, he swung round in the swivel chair and took in the room's sparse furnishings.

"Better than the visits hall," I told him.

"Cool," he said.

Things with Darren as I discovered were generally 'sweet' or 'cool'.

He wasn't a big talker at the best of times and the Chaplaincy setting hadn't changed that. At the end of the visit, Darren had a last admiring look in the mirror. If he stood some way from it, he could admire his designer tee shirt from different angles. He adjusted his jeans, took a final look at the tee shirt and got ready to leave.

"See you next week then, Darren." He nodded.

"Sweet," he said.

Chapter 37

Phone calls are not easy in prison. They're expensive. Things can go wrong. Men can have bad phone calls as well as bad visits. Making up for things said, trying to mend a relationship, just finding the right words when time is limited can be tricky under normal circumstances. In prison, it can become impossible. It's certainly never easy.

For Ronnie, it was different. His call was a happy one. It was happy for him but not for me. It was his first visit to the Chaplaincy and it could have been my last visit. After a quick look round, his eyes lit up when he spotted the telephone.

"Could you phone my gran for me, miss?"

"Sorry. I'm afraid not. We're not allowed to do anything like that."

"I could do it, miss. Only take a minute."

"No, you don't understand, it's not allowed at all. It's against the rules. It's just for Chaplaincy use."

Ronnie was young but very determined. He was not going to take no for an answer. It all happened so quickly. I had no idea he would move so fast. The phone was in his hand before I could do anything about it. He seemed to get an outside line immediately. In seconds, he was dialling the number. The door of the Chaplaincy office was closed, always was during visits, but there was another office next door to ours which was occupied. An officer had just escorted inmates to the Bible study group on the same landing. He could still be there for all I knew. I was horrified. Apart from trying to snatch the phone from Ronnie's hand, I couldn't think how to stop him. Luckily, his call was brief. He had little to say on visits but talking to his gran was a gift for him.

"You all right, gran? I'm all right. You all right? Yeah, I'm alright as well."

This call was hardly a matter of life and death. In a couple of minutes, Ronnie had run out of steam.

He looked delighted. I was nerve-wracked.

Could have been the end of visiting for me but Ronnie had no idea of this. He was beaming.

"Thanks, miss," he said. "That was great."

I kept thinking a call would come through from the switchboard asking what that was about. Eventually, it was time for him to go back to the wing.

I decided to sit quietly for a moment before leaving for home.

Chapter 38

I've been asked what I get to talk about on these visits. Well, mostly it's the men who talk and I listen. Gradually, some kind of link is established between us. Visitors have to be guarded on anything which would identify them. They don't even give their last name – Even then and in an unnatural environment where everything has to be locked and unlocked, it can still feel normal. Just two people sitting together

One night, on my way in to visit Peter, my car lights started giving me a problem. Only side lights or full beam worked. This was new to me. I wasn't keen on night driving and felt nervous. Other drivers were flashing their lights before I realised what the problem was. I was relieved when I arrived at my visit and launched into the story. This was a story which took up a good part of the visit.

"Garage will fix it," Peter told.me. "It can happen. Same as a light bulb at home going."

Each time I visited, he brought up the subject again, telling me I would be all right going home.

"Won't happen again," he assured me.

Since the visitor is limited on what he or she can reveal about their life, it helps if I can bring up something from the outside world, no matter how ordinary. The prison regime runs on the same lines day after day. The usual answer to, 'so what's happening. How is it going' is inevitably.

'Oh, you know. Same old, same old.'

Small things help. The failure of my car lights carried over to a couple of visits. At one visit, I realised I'd left my mobile at home. Since I was driving at night, I generally checked I had it in my car. Not this time. After that, I was asked at the end of each visit,

"You've got your phone this time, miss. You'll be all right then."

The highlight of my domestic stories was that returning from a visit one night, I went through a speed camera. The inmate I was visited was delighted when I told him. I couldn't see why but it certainly entertained him.

I was delayed going in one evening since there was an incident in the prison. Being prison, no one tells you how long it will be or what it's about. It dragged on and I was concerned it would cut into visiting time or I wouldn't be allowed in at all. Also it was a long boring wait.

"What a waste of time," I told my visitee.

"It can be hard getting into this place."

"It can be hard getting out, miss," he said

I was asked by an inmate on one visit what friends thought of me visiting.

"Very little," I said. That was certainly true.

I admitted that my daughter worried about me a bit, especially when I said it was now one to one visiting.

"She thinks that must be dangerous," I explained.

"Tell her there's an emergency button," he said.

I must have looked a bit vague since I looked around the walls but couldn't see anything.

"You don't know where it is, do you, miss?"

He kindly pointed it out to me.

Just odd moments when you could almost be in the real world.

Chapter 39

Visits can be difficult for different reasons. When the only information you have are a person's name and his prison number, it's hard to tell in advance how things will go. When someone is really uncommunicative, it's definitely a struggle. It's not easy to keep conversation going during the visit when the person cannot find anything to say. That makes for a very long hour. The first time I came across this, I couldn't help asking myself. Why would he want a visit in the first place? Mostly, it is because it gets a man out of his cell and off the wing. The chance of moving into a different part of the prison and being with someone who shows an interest in you could be another part of it.

Although there is no training for visiting, I tried keeping in mind the one piece of advice I had been given. Remember that making conversation doesn't come easily to these men. It's not something they are used to doing. A little less difficult than this laboured kind of visit is with someone who cannot stop talking at all. I only met one prisoner like that. This was not a conversation between two people. This was more like a stream of consciousness. There was no gap for me to intervene with a question or comment. Under those circumstances, the most I could do was throw in a 'really' or 'goodness me' when he seemed to be slowing down. I presumed, on our first visit, this was some kind of nervousness. Not so. Towards the end of our visits and just before he was released, I think I understood why he talked like that. He was definitely facing a lot of problems on release. I reckoned this was his way of going over these problems again and again as though things might become clearer to him. Maybe the constant repetition would afford him some kind of solution.

The most difficult – and one of the saddest visits I ever had – was with a prisoner who had suffered a stroke. This had happened a few years previously and in a different prison. It had not only affected his speech, making him difficult to understand, but his memory. Simple questions such as, where are you from, or how long have you been in here, brought the same answers. There would be a pause and then he would reply 'I don't know' or 'I don't remember'. His fellow prisoners did not mix with him. I suppose they just found it too hard going or they had enough problems of their own. I asked him if he borrowed any of the books from the library. He wandered around and picked up two which he showed me. They were comics of a sort but without even the simplest captions. Since this library was quite well stocked, I took it that he could not read. Another result of the stroke, perhaps. It was difficult to understand why someone with this degree of disability would be in a prison environment.

I only once visited a prisoner who was on the Health Wing. Having no idea what a prison's Health Wing would be like I imagined a normal kind of hospital environment. I thought the prisoner/patient might be in a small ward with other men or in a single room. Nothing could have been further from the truth. It was physically the most uncomfortable visit I ever had.

An officer escorted me along corridors to a part of the prison I didn't recognise. The prisoner was in a room on his own but behind a locked door. I was not allowed to go into the room since there were not enough officers to keep an eye on things. Security, again. I had to stand in the corridor, trying to communicate with this inmate through a small window in the door of his room. It was a very painful hour since it meant standing close enough to the door to be able to see him through this small window. This window was so oddly situated near the top of the door that I could hardly make out what his room was like. He stood for some of the visit and then went back to sitting on the edge of his bed.

I don't know what the point of it was for him since, giving this set up, talk was minimal. Every now and then, I had to stand on tiptoe peering into this room. Less than half way into the 'visit', my back began to ache and my feet hurt. I could not work out why anyone thought that was a reasonable way to visit someone. If it was difficult for me, it was probably worse for him I was never more relieved to see the approach of a prison officer.

"Right," he said, indicating our time was up.

He escorted me out of the Health Wing, my one and only visit there.

Chapter 40

Gerald set the record straight on his first visit, although I think I would have worked it out anyway. The way he dressed, the way he spoke and his body language spelled it out.

He had hardly sat down before he announced, "Hello, Christine. I'm Gerald. I'm gay."

His introduction was done in such a matter of fact way, I couldn't think of an immediate response. It struck me he had taken the trouble to know my Christian name. That was a change from being addressed as miss.

His clothes were a long way from the prison issue of tracksuit bottoms and sloppy sweater. They definitely looked different and expensive. It wasn't his sexual orientation which was of any interest to me, although the need to spell it out, especially in a prison environment, I found strange. He didn't seem like someone who had been in prison before. There was something in the way he conducted himself which suggested that he had wandered into this environment by mistake.

He was very relaxed, excellent company, telling me all about his partner and where they lived. He had brought over photographs from the wing both of his partner and their flat to show me. That in itself was unusual. He told me that his partner had already visited and they had telephone conversations every day. Everything about Gerald set him apart from his surroundings.

What concerned me about him was, given how he had introduce himself, how he would be treated inside, I wasn't sure quite how to put it but he quickly set me straight.

"I get on easily with people. I wouldn't have expected any problem."

"I thought, maybe because you are gay and so open about it, people might…"

"No, not at all," he assured me.

"But a prison environment is surely different," I said

"There are at least two men on my wing who are gay and share a cell," he told me.

I presumed they were together to prevent trouble from a cellmate who was straight. Gerald took it that homosexuality was accepted in prison and gave no one any problem.

Although he was open about his lifestyle, he was vague about his offence. He told me his job had involved handling large amounts of cash and something had gone wrong there. That, whatever it was, would be sorted out, he told me and he expected an early release. This was his first time inside and he seemed intrigued by what he was learning.

He couldn't believe that men were using drugs where officers could see them.

"I was horrified," he said.

He was also horrified by the level of literacy among prisoners. Already, he was helping his cellmate with reading and writing. I think he looked at his time inside as a learning experience. One or two officers had been helpful to him, he told me so he would send them a thank you note on release. I reckoned that would definitely be a first.

He acted like some kind of observer of prison life. As far as my experience of prison visiting went, my short time with Gerald was both different and unexpected.

Chapter 41

I discovered that prison is a melting pot of religious faiths. The thinking is that whatever a prisoner's faith is, he should have access to a minister of that faith, be it Sikh, Buddhist, Muslim, Anglican, Jewish, Quaker or any other.

Anything which gets a prisoner out of his cell and off the wing is welcome. He might come over for the Bible group, attend Chapel on Sunday for the C of E service or Saturday for Mass. That might be because of his religious faith or because it gives him a chance to meet mates from other wings. Since visitors do not bring up the subject of religion during visits, it would be hard to say which is the greater draw. I was told that prisoners were asking for rosaries but since they generally called them 'rosemarys', I don't think it was taken too seriously by the chaplain. Some prisoners wore these rosary beads round their neck. That didn't signify they were Catholic, since that's not how Catholics use the rosary, but who knows.

Men can be baptised in prison, married in prison or instructed in the faith of their choice in prison. Just by chance, I once discussed arranging a marriage in prison which was not something I expected to do. I had answered the Chaplaincy phone while I waited for my visit to start. Any other time, I ignored it when it rang since it could only be Chaplaincy business. This time, it rang once, rang off and then rang again, so I answered. I explained right away I wasn't the person to speak to, that I had only answered the phone since there was no Chaplaincy person around and I wouldn't be able to help but that didn't stop the caller. She sounded very young and excited but when she said, "It's about the wedding arrangements," I just wanted her to stop. I had no idea how these things worked and I knew I wouldn't be able to help her.

She seemed desperate to lay it all on someone and that was me – the wrong person. All I could do was note down her name and telephone number, leaving that for the chaplain. It felt so intrusive since she was such a mixture of nervousness and excitement. What was meant to be the happiest day of your life was being celebrated in prison. I would like to have sounded happy for her but I don't know if I did. I rounded it off with wishing her the best of luck and left a detailed note for the Chaplain.

Chapter 42

I knew Michael had children since at one visit, he promised to bring me pictures of them from his cell. He never got round to that and never said much about his family. He was also vague about visits he got from his wife. "It's difficult for her to get in," he told me. "The thing is getting someone to watch the kids. Anyway, she works part time."

This was a hall visit so I made a point of looking around at the children running around in and out of the various tables.

"She could bring them in with her," I suggested.

He looked at me as though I didn't understand.

"Why would I want my kids to see me in here?" he asked. "Why would anyone want to do that?"

For a moment, we both looked around at the other visitors. The smaller children were being looked after by the crèche provided by the prison and run by volunteers. The older children were sharing the visit with their mums.

Since there were babies in arms as well as children of school age, I mumbled something about other people doing it.

He just shook his head and I wished the subject hadn't come up. It was a quieter visit than normal when there was always some chat about anything happening on his wing. It was the first time I had put some thought to the decisions these men had to make about visiting. The choice was of seeing their children, making it clear why dad was absent from home or maybe concocting some story to explain his absence.

Looking around at children of school age, I wondered, not for the first time, how they squared their absence from school or indeed, what they told friends. I think I could understand why wives and girlfriends, who had children, made only irregular visits

When the visits were over, with much kissing and hugging between dads and children, Michael sat stony faced until it was time for him to go.

I wished I hadn't broached the subject. I should have left our vague talks about family as they were. It taught me to be more careful in future. He was transferred to another establishment shortly after, whether that was further from home or nearer, I never found out.

Chapter 43

Although visitors are all doing the same thing, we take different things from our visits and learn to handle them as best we can. There is no 'one size fits all' to visiting

One of our long-serving visitors confessed it was a bit of a mystery to him. He wasn't referring to visiting itself but what he asked himself after a visit – Why would a young guy like that want to see an old codger like me. The old codger was in his 50s but I could see what he meant. Sadly, young people don't seem attracted to prison visiting.

One of the women visitors, in her 60s, thought her visits had started off well, until the third visit. She was suddenly told by her visitee that it would be better if she visited someone else. She was puzzled by this since her visits had been going well. She later learned, through another visitor, that the young man had been embarrassed by one of the other men asking him 'is that your new girlfriend then'. Luckily, visitors take these things in their stride.

I heard of one visitor who was offered a marriage proposal. The prisoner had some problem with immigration and was threatened with deportation so having a British wife would help. She politely declined.

Another visitor had, literally, the same conversation every single week she came in. Not easy, since the visits went on for a few months. "It was like hearing the same record over and over again," she said. I have no idea how she handled that.

Hard to say what makes a good prison visitor, but a sense of humour definitely helps.

Chapter 44

"You'll like Nick," I was told. "He could charm the birds from the trees."

The Liaison officer who had arranged the visit, added, "He is very good looking. I could fall in love with him myself. If I was 30 years younger, that is."

Nick was certainly as she described him.

He greeted me with a warm handshake, an even warmer smile and a kiss on the cheek which was unusual on a first visit. He chatted easily, asking me about myself (which didn't often happen in visits) and made the time fly. Towards the end of the visit, he became nostalgic about his life outside and what he missed about it.

"Tell you what I really miss and what I'd love," he said. "Chocolate, a big bar of chocolate. Oh, I miss that. I love the one with nuts and raisins in it, wrapped in tinfoil. It's the best. I've really missed that since I've been in here. I'll definitely be buying one of them when I get out of here."

He was probably in his early 20's but he sounded like a child.

He gave me a warm hug before an officer appeared to tell me time was up.

I took a bar of chocolate to him at my next visit. I thought he might start eating it during the visit but he was obviously going to enjoy it in his cell. He hid it down the waistband of his jeans which gave me a twinge of conscience since I realised then this must be against the rules. But, honestly, I told myself on the way home – a bar of chocolate. How can that be considered contraband. What can be the problem?

I learned the following week that it wasn't just the fruit and nut which he was missing. I was telling one of the

Chaplaincy team about my visit which I thought was funny but I could see she wasn't amused by it.

"You've given a prisoner chocolate which had," she paused, "tinfoil in it?"

My first lesson in drug use.

Chapter 45

When a prisoner is a bit hazy about the role of a prison visitor, I have to put them straight. No, I am not a social worker, no I do not get paid, no, I am not from any religious group. Once that is sorted, things are straightforward. Only once I had a visit with someone who thought I was there to offer him practical help.

His name was Gareth. There was no 'hello' or a handshake from him, just an immediate pouring out of his problems. He needed help in every direction and he assumed that's why I was visiting. He told me that his wife had left him so on release, he would have nowhere to go. He had been told she was moving to another area but he had no idea where. What clothes he had were with her in the flat they had shared. I learned on subsequent visits and from other visitors, this was a problem which came up frequently. If a relationship broke down, the prisoner could lose contact not just with an ex-partner but with what clothes and possessions he had on the outside. Gareth was due for release shortly and he thought I could be of some practical help. It all came tumbling out. Could I help him with accommodation? What could he do about clothes since he only had what he was wearing? Once he paused, I explained that wasn't what I was about. I just visited. I couldn't help him with any of these things.

"I've only got the clothes I came in with," he said. "You must be able to help me with that."

"I'm sorry," I said. "There's nothing I can do. I'm just a visitor."

He must have thought if he persisted long enough, I would come up with something. Communication had fallen through somewhere. He had the wrong idea about my visit. I don't know how that could have happened. Once he realised I could be of no help, he sat back and stopped talking. We must have been the only silent couple in the visits hall. There was no point in me just sitting there since he never said another word. Eventually, I went over to one of the officers and blurted out the story.

"There's no point in me staying here, I told him. I cannot be of any help to him. He doesn't realise I am just a visitor." The Officer agreed to escort me out. I went over to Gareth, said I was sorry he had the wrong idea, but he just shook his head.

I felt awful for him and completely useless. That was nothing compared to what he must have been feeling. No one could explain why that had happened. I prayed that nothing like that would ever come up again.

Chapter 46

Visitors, as well as prisoners, must abide by the rules of the prison. These are covered by the blanket word 'security'. Sally had been visiting each week for over a year when her visits came to an end. Being a Quaker, she knew how much Quakers had contributed to prison reform. She was a very committed visitor. Young Joseph, as she referred to him, had just been transferred to another prison. He was young, a first time offender with the usual problems, but he assured Sally her visits had helped him. They had got on well but this all comes to a halt when a prisoner is transferred. She wished him well for the future and hoped he would settle down at his new establishment. Whether their move is to another prison or they are released, the visitor is always hopeful things will go well. A handshake or a hug, plus a joking kind of warning, 'I don't want to see you in here again' is the end of it. Sally's case was different. Young Joseph's new abode was in an area further north where her married son and family lived. *Why not check up on how he's doing,* she thought. Maybe the next time she visited her son, she could see Joseph and find out how his new place was working out or him.

She contacted the chaplain at the prison, explained that she would be in the area and had been Joseph's visitor, would it be possible on her next trip North to visit Joseph. That was fine, he agreed so a visit for Joseph was arranged. But somehow, news got back. Sally was informed she had broken the rules and could no longer be a prison visitor – at any prison. This was a blanket ban.

She presumed this was a mistake or some misunderstanding which could be cleared up. She explained how it had been arranged with the prison chaplain, that it seemed a good idea since she was in the area, but to no effect.

She demanded an explanation and wrote all this in detail to the Governor. I wrote a back-up letter. She told her story to anyone who would listen, but she was up against a brick wall. Security. She had broken the rules. She wouldn't let it go and asked for some kind of explanation of why she was banned since her visit to Joseph had been agreed by that prison's chaplain. She was eventually told that her actions in visiting Joseph in a new establishment suggested co-dependency.

"I couldn't believe what they were saying," she told me. "Co-dependency... I'm old enough to be his grandmother."

Worse was to follow. Apart from visiting, Sally did a few hours in education with some of the lads. When her rule breaking came to light, an officer entered the class and escorted her immediately from the prison.

So no more visiting, no more helping the lads with literacy. She went through various stages of being non-plussed at the prison's decision and then anger, especially at the way it had been handled. Nothing helped and none of it made sense. She had come up against a brick wall. Her feelings of frustration and disappointment that her visiting days were over, eventually, petered out, but it took a long time.

I met her a few years later and while I worked out where we had met, her first words, apart from 'how are you' were,

"Remember, I'm the visitor who..." and in the middle of the Waitrose car park, we went over it all again.

Chapter 47

Prison is a harsh environment. Life inside is run on a set of rules. Locking and unlocking is the order of the day. How else could it be with over 1000 men locked up and having to be kept under some kind of control. Nevertheless, seeing a prison van drive in and, later, its inmates being processed and introduced, to a new way of life, makes a bleak picture for the onlooker. The vans with their blacked-out windows are commonly referred to as sweat boxes. Anyone I have asked about this, tells me they are well named. A long journey in one of these, whether from Court or another prison doesn't leave much to the imagination.

Sharing a limited space with a stranger whom you know nothing about is the start of adapting to prison. Visitors are not there to question the ins and outs of the justice system or be judgmental. They are just there to listen to someone but apart from hearing some unhappy stories, I discovered there is also a chance to witness acts of kindness.

I had seen Paul, from a travelling family, in the Chapel on one or two occasions. I didn't know him so had no idea that he was epileptic. There are always at least two officers sitting at the back of the Chapel, so I suppose one of them would have known what to do, but on this occasion, before they saw what was happening, his mates were looking after Paul. I expect they had seen him in a fit before. They got him to his feet, stroked his back, smoothed his clothes down and spoke to him. There were a few congratulatory pats on the back as well as calls of 'you all right now, Paul,' until he was himself again. That was the first time I had been close to anyone having a seizure. I wouldn't have had any idea what to do. Obviously, they did but it was the concerned way they did it until he recovered which intrigued me.

Small things like leaving bits and pieces to your cell mate or some friend on another wing, happens when someone is released. These are only bits of toiletry or a few tea bags which would seem nothing to anyone on the outside. For an inmate who really needs them, it makes a big difference.

The reaction when a mate has been given their release date, or knows he is going on to an open prison, raises the spirits, as does any good news of family shared with another prisoner. These are small acts of kindness which would hardly be commented upon on the outside. Under prison conditions, they mean a great deal.

Chapter 48

It's not surprising that there are men in prison with varying health problems, mental as well as physical. There are also some men with really low IQs. When Pete told me he had joined the book group in the prison, I thought that would give us something to talk about. Until then, his conversation had been limited. On our next visit, I raised the subject and, yes, he had enjoyed it.

"It's good," he told me. "It gets me off the wing."

Anything that gets a man off the wing is considered a good thing. Pete's cell mate was going to the group as well which was company for him. Apparently, there had been five or six of them there and the good news was that you were allowed to keep the book under discussion.

"What was it about?" I asked.

"What?" asked Pete.

"The book."

"I can't remember," he said.

"Never mind. I thought maybe I had read it. What was it called?"

This was a question too far Pete but it let me know that the book group was not going to stimulate our conversations.

He moved his hands around vaguely and then said, "It had a kind of blue cover on it."

I was only once asked by an inmate to read a letter to him. I was trying to get through a group of inmates who were being moved from one wing to another. Suddenly, one of them was asking 'could you read this for me, miss,' pushing a sheet of paper into my hand. I felt embarrassed on his behalf and when I realised that it was badly written with some weird misspellings difficult to decipher, I knew this was going to be hard work. I didn't get far with it since there was quite a bit of jostling among the men and suddenly, the group started moving. I just had time to push the letter back into his hand and he started to move off.

"Thanks, miss," he called out.

Chapter 49

Antony suffered from Attention Deficit Syndrome which did nothing for the conversation during our visit. We were in one of the Chaplaincy rooms so there was plenty of scope for straightening things out there. Antony did just that for the duration of the visit which I found nerve-wracking and put paid to any kind of conversation. He straightened up anything which was on the desk, papers, files, books, anything which was in his line of vision. Then he did it again and again.

This was just part of visiting and gave no real problem. What did was seeing signs of self-harm in the person you're visiting. Occasionally, it is obvious that the scars are old. On one visit, I could see these on both arms of the inmate. They were hard to ignore, although he didn't seem upset when he realised I was looking at them. I thought it was a sad sight, but he just shrugged it off.

Certain things said in conversation can be seen as danger signs. Suicide or attempted suicide happens in prison, so when a prisoner says, 'I cannot be doing with this anymore. I've had enough,' the question is this. Is he just fed up and having a bad day or is there more to it than that? The advice to the visitor is if you are at all concerned, to report it. Fortunately, I never visited anyone who showed a real desire to end his life or even make an attempt. I did visit a prisoner who had found his cell mate attempting suicide during the night. He had to press the emergency bell in their cell and make an attempt to get the man down.

Chapter 50

My stint selling snacks in the visits centre added another dimension to visiting. I was aware that some of the inmates were far from home. They told me it was hard for family to visit regularly and it could mean travelling by public transport. Not easy with young children in tow.

The staff do what they can helping out, especially for new visitors. There are visitors who arrive late and are afraid they might lose their visit so they panic. There are always some who have brought the wrong ID. Other visitors think the ID doesn't apply to small children. New visitors seem wary and generally, look tired, especially if they have brought children with them. Young girls, on the other hand, including those who are pregnant look eternally optimistic.

Since I am only seen as cafe staff, I am rarely asked for any help. The one time I was approached, it was an object lesson in itself. The couple were foreign nationals and for some reason, they had brought their luggage into the centre. Maybe they had come by public transport or they figured bringing it into the centre was safer than being left in their car. They looked completely bewildered. They didn't seem to want any refreshments but looked at me as though I might be the one person who could help them.

Although their English was quite good, I couldn't work out what their travelling arrangements had been. The man, in his fifties, told me he had come to see his son. He showed me money he had brought him, thinking he could take it into the visit. I had to explain he couldn't do that and the best place would be in the locker. He and his wife looked so unsure, so puzzled, it was obvious they had never been in this situation before. I told them when their number was called, they would just walk over to the prison gate. I tried explaining to them about the security they would go through and assured them it was quite straight forward. There would be no problem. "Nothing to worry about," I told them. I hoped later I hadn't painted too rosy a picture for them.

Although they looked a bit more assured, they obviously thought I was the one person to hold on to. I couldn't tell them my job was only to sell refreshments since they seemed to see me as some kind of official figure. I told the other volunteer that she would have to hold the fort on her own for a short while. When their number was called, I ushered them out and walked them across the yard to the gate. If the visits centre was an alien place to them, the sight of the prison building would be more so. It felt like lambs to the slaughter. I couldn't go further than the date with them since I didn't have a V.O. I wasn't sure how much they took on board but I kept emphasising how straight forward it was from then on and how helpful everyone would be.

How it went with their son, I had no idea. Their money was safely locked away, minus the £7 I told them they could take over to buy refreshments for him. I had left for home before the end of their visit so I never found out how that went for them.

Chapter 51

For obvious reasons, no one in prison looks forward to Christmas – unless their release date means they will be home in time. Reactions vary. Some men prefer to stay in their cells. For others, it's the time to settle old scores so violence breaks out on the wings. As one inmate put it to me – who wants someone wishing you a Happy Christmas when you are in here. Anything is better than that. Phone calls home at that time can make absence from home even harder to bear. Hard for the men, hard for the families and hard for the officers. "They just want to 'kick off'," an officer told me. Everyone is glad when it's over.

The Carol Service arranged by the Chaplaincy each year has a mixed response. There is nothing worse than enforced jollity when you feel really down so some of the men don't bother to come over. Local dignitaries are always invited giving them a chance to talk to the men and hopefully lighten the atmosphere. A small choir has been rounded up from the braver souls and one or two 'volunteers' amongst them give some of the readings. It gives prison visitors a chance to chat to their visitee and, sometimes awkwardly, be introduced to some of their mates.

Mince pies and cups of tea in a relaxed atmosphere, and then back to their cells ready in most cases to batten down the hatches and be grateful that all of it will soon be over.

Chapter 52

Rules change in prison. The changes affect prison visitors as well as the men they visit. When I began visiting, certain things were allowed. I was able to buy trainers on one occasion as well as sending in something for Christmas. Cards for birthdays and other occasions were also acceptable. Whether visiting in the hall or on a one to one basis in the Chaplaincy, the visit started with a handshake, a hug or a kiss on the cheek. It never occurred to me that things which were once acceptable would suddenly become unacceptable and all without explanation. My first experience was an attempt to send a book in to a prisoner. "Cannot do that," I was told. "Rules have changed."

My reaction was 'what on earth for' but there is no arguing with rule changes. Generally, the only answer is 'security'.

It was Pauline's experience on her visit to the hall which brought things home to me. It was all over a kiss – or rather a kiss which never happened. At the end of her visit, an officer reported that a kiss had been exchanged between visitor and inmate. "Absolutely not," Pauline said. "That never happened." She was indignant and couldn't believe what was being said. She presumed her word would be taken on that, but not so. She appealed to the Governor and any source she could think of but her word was not accepted. Worse was to follow. The incident was put on the prisoner's Probation Report and, despite complaining to the Governor on his behalf, that was it. She pursued the matter but got nowhere with it.

A long term visitor trying to console her said,
"There was a time, Pauline, that would have been ok but rules change."

That was no consolation to Pauline especially when the 'misdemeanour' had never taken place.

Chapter 53

It's cushy in there. The general public know that for a certainty. They've read it in the press. Otherwise, they argue why would they go back in.

Of course they go back in. However much they swear it to their prison visitor – and to their families – they return. I've seen a familiar face, catching my eye, either looking a bit sheepish or putting on a brave face on more than one occasion. Often, it's over a missed Probation visit. Either that or they have committed some minor misdemeanour which pulls them back in

For most, it's just hard to cope on the outside. They genuinely do not want to come back to prison but without support or back up, it's sometimes inevitable. Families have broken up, relationships have broken down. Their old mates are still around, the ones ready to offer them 'a little bit of stuff' to help them out. And that's the start of their road back inside.

Their life inside, whether cushy or not, has been structured. They're locked and unlocked at set times, given three meals and with a bit of luck if you keep your head down, you can do it, I've been told more than once. And, anyway, as the mantra goes, 'if you can't do the time, don't do the crime'. That's fine but after the security of prison life, the outside world without any help or support can seem a daunting place.

It surprised me at first that men I visited were so nervous in the days leading up to their release. There was no 'I cannot wait to get out. It's going to be great'. It was mostly uncertainty, especially when it got nearer to the date. They are given a travel warrant, some cash and if they have no holdall they can be given a prison bag. This can be a black bag stamped HMP, just in case there is some doubt about where he has come from. Our Prison Visitor Association heard from a Governor, whom we had invited as a speaker, that he had seen a young fellow, obviously recently released, on a rail station platform carrying a bag with HMP stamped on it. He was horrified on behalf of the offender. I was horrified that he had reached Governor status and was unaware that was how the system worked.

No job prospects, a criminal record and an uncertain future. Unless they are very fortunate, they have no on to meet them at the gate.

A Probation officer painted the picture for me.

"Their life in here has been organised all during their sentence. They don't have to think for themselves. They don't have to make any decisions. Suddenly, they are on the out and they are simply not prepared. That starts as soon as they get out of the gate. They might meet up with old mates in the pub and before they know it, their money is spent. Not clever, I know. It's a kind of bravado in front of mates or the feeling that a drink will help them."

He cannot expect any help from his prison visitor. That is against the rules, so just a few parting words –

"Hope it goes well," and a jokey –

"Don't want to see you in here again, do I?"

Chapter 54

Looking back is maybe not a good idea. Many of the changes in prison visiting since I started ten years ago have seemed nit picking to me. What harm could there be in sending a prisoner a book or a note wishing him luck on his release? For visitors whose experience goes back a lot longer, the changes have been huge. Sitting chatting, or listening, to a prisoner in his cell was, at one time, the accepted thing. I learned there was even a time, many years ago, when you could entertain a discharged prisoner in your home. I felt there was a time when the relaxation of the rules would have meant much to the prisoner. I never thought that the changes in the prison system would affect me as a prison visitor. Indeed, the changes have brought my days as a prison visitor to an end.

Changes to the prison core day mean that prisoners are locked up much earlier in the evening. That and the fall in prison staffing levels has made it difficult to carry on with evening visiting in the Chaplaincy. As a result, some visitors have called it a day when their evening visiting came to an end. Afternoon visiting in the visits hall didn't suit everyone. My one to one visits in the Chaplaincy where we could meet in a more normal surrounding than the visits hall were a privilege for both visitor and inmate. I was eternally grateful for that.

Since I visit in the Chaplaincy rather than the hall, my days inside are now over. It was unexpected so it comes as a bit of a blow. For me, I cannot think of anything which would be as rewarding.

I'll miss so much about it. So much of it surprised me. As the men have said to me – 'it's a different world in here, miss'. As other visitors comment regularly – mostly when they are exasperated about some change in rules –get used to it, it's not like the real world, is it.

It's certainly a different world and I'm grateful to have learned something about it. I didn't expect the men I met would be so frank. There was certainly no show of bravado when they spoke of their crime. If you can't do the time, don't do the crime, as they say. Only on the rare occasion did I visit anyone who excused their offence. I met many who deeply regretted what they had done. With one exception, I never met any who boasted about it.

I was never Stewart's visitor. I just got to know him slightly through Bible meetings in the Chaplaincy. I often had to hang about on the fringes of their meetings while I waited for my visit to get underway. He came over as a quiet, gentle soul and one that the men in his group genuinely liked. He had killed someone and served a long sentence for that. At the end of his sentence, he was allowed out on a tag. I was there when the other men showed how pleased they were for him. They congratulated him, wished him the best and said things like –

"You never deserved to be in here, Stewart."

He shook his head.

"Yes, I did. Someone is dead because of me. Don't ever forget that."

Chapter 55

It was the first time I realised prison had its own language which I mostly heard from the inmates I visited. Any conversation with officers was rare and monosyllabic. When I started visiting one said to me –
"Draw keys?"
I had just shown him my ID and been asked –
"Do you have a mobile, any personal objects apart from ID?"
Then again –
"Draw keys?"
My mind went blank for a moment and then a volunteer following me in, told him, "Yes, she drew keys."
She signed herself in, then attached a bunch of keys to the belt round her waist. When I discovered how many gates she had to lock and unlock before we arrived at the Chaplaincy, plus the rules about anyone else locking and unlocking from the opposite direction, I knew drawing keys was not for me.
It found it easy to fall into prison terminology. When a prisoner leaves the establishment, he is 'shipped out'. Being moved to an open mean he is leaving a secure prison for one where there is more freedom – of a sort. The idea is to prepare him for his eventual release, providing he fits the criteria for going to an open. Once there, he finds that his cell is now referred go as his room, and locking and unlocking no longer applies. Once there, he is given the opportunity of working outside and returning to the open at the end of his working day. It sounds promising except that after the regime of a closed prison, some find this sudden kind of freedom hard to handle. It's easy to abscond (you 'abscond from an open but 'escape' from a closed prison) but pointless since once caught, he is sent back to a closed prison. The taste of a kind of freedom, in an open has its pitfalls for some.

When released from prison, he might have to be 'on the tag' an electronic device which tracks his movement. Like an open, that too sounds like a step in the right direction but that semi kind of freedom has its temptations as well.

- Prison vans which are used to bring in inmates or take them to Court are commonly referred to as 'sweat boxes'. According to anyone with experience of them, they are aptly named. As with police officers, prison officers are given different definitions – the most polite being 'screws'.
- Getting a negative result when you appear before a Board for one reason or another is always getting 'a knock back'. An incident generally means a disturbance of one kind or another. Sadly, it can also be used when there has 'been a suicide. The first time I heard it used in that context, I felt shocked that someone's death, especially in a prison cell could be referred to as 'an incident'. Of course, for the officers, it has to be treated as one with procedures to be followed. The effect on whoever is first on the scene cannot be imagined.

Chapter 56

I've been asked what has it been like going into prison regularly. I've been asked if I'm not afraid being so near to 'these men' and I can truthfully tell them that no, I never have been. I have never seen why I should be. I've been more nervous in a town centre on a Saturday night and anyway, depending where you are, there is an officer presence. They are anxious to know if I'm told what their crime is. Once again, no, since I am not interested and it doesn't affect how I feel about who I'm visiting.

Do you find out if they have re-offended and are back in prison? Rarely. Am I allowed to see them on the outside? Definitely not. Do I choose who I am going to visit? No, I am given a name and a number, and arrange a visit. Generally, I send them a card first, explaining the procedure and asking them to let the Chaplaincy know if they have a problem with any of that. I would like to know if they have changed their mind for some reason since that would save a wasted trip for me. Since nothing is as organised as that in prison, I have had more than one wasted visit. That means, arriving for a visit then turning the car around and driving back home again. There's rarely an explanation for that.

A more difficult question, or the one I find hardest is – Do you think your visiting has done anyone any good? Was there really a point to it? Has it made any difference? Well, it has made a difference to me, but for the men I have visited, no, I wouldn't think so. Of course, I have no idea although I know visiting the same person for a long period was better than a very short acquaintance. Even that is hard to equate since one inmate I saw only twice ended the second visit (his last) with a very enthusiastic, 'I'll never forget you, miss,' which was very cheering if a bit unlikely. Generally, these visits have just given them a chance to get off the Wing and speak freely to someone. They cannot be like that with other prisoners or officers. The first-time inmates are unsure how to approach an officer when they have a problem. Older men have told me 'you always have to watch your back on the wings'.

One explaining how it was for him, said, "I make sure younger guys know I'm not to be messed with, otherwise, they try to make life difficult for me. They want to impress their mates. Best to put them right from the start."

Chapter 57

I realised from my start of visiting that few people, either family or friends, are interested in what it's like to visit. Coming to the end of my visiting, I decided to do a straw poll going over the questions I was asked and ones I wished I had asked them.

Why should they expect people like you to visit them when they must have family and friends?

Well, some men have no family visits for different reasons. Men can find themselves in prison a long way from home so it might be physically difficult for family to visit. Their families may have given up on them. If they are regular offenders, the attitude might be 'enough is enough'. Some men cannot handle their nearest and dearest seeing them inside. Some particularly do not want their children to see them in prison. A man can have a prison visitor see them whether they have family visits or not. They can expose their feelings or say things to a prison visitor they would find hard to do to a family member. A prison visitor is completely objective so there's no fear of recrimination.

Are you not afraid of being close to someone who has committed a crime when you go inside the prison?

I never have been, not even on my first visit. I would not be doing it if I thought there was something frightening about it. For one thing, it would hardly be in the interest of an inmate to do anything foolish. For another, in the visits hall, there are officers in attendance. In all the time I visited, I never heard of one of our visitors coming to harm. In the Chaplaincy set up there are emergency buttons on the wall. Having said that, I did have to have one pointed out to me by a prisoner.

Are the men you visit foreign or British? There are men from various ethnic backgrounds. Anyone who is illegally in the country is usually awaiting deportation.

Are you told what their crime if before you visit them? No, although I could find out if I wanted to but it's not of any interest to a visitor. It doesn't affect how you visit.

Allowed to see them afterwards? No and for security reasons, all they know about me is my first name. I can only remember one of them using it. For some reason, it was always 'miss'.

I don't find out if they have re-offended. If they have, they might be housed in another prison so I wouldn't see them anyway. It's not something I would be told.

Can I choose who I want to visit?

No, we have a Visitors Association who collate a number of prisoners who say they would like a visit. The number of visitors waiting are then given one of that number

What do they do all day? That depends on the regime of the prison. Normally, they are unlocked by about 8 am. Their breakfast, cereals mainly, have been given to them the night before. They eat it in their cell. If they have been given work on the wing, they do that. That can be in the kitchen, laundry or just cleaning the wings. They are locked up again and given some food for lunch time. They are locked and unlocked at different times during the day, but unless it's an establishment where there is education and various courses to go on, they spend a lot of time locked up. They watch a lot of TV since there is little else to do. They are locked up early evening, once again, depending on that prison's regime. They are locked up until the next morning when the same day happens again. A bit like Groundhog day. The common answer to 'how has your day been' is a shrug and 'same old, same old'.

How do officers react to you as an official visitor?

Mainly, they don't. I have never been sure what they think of prison visitors since there has never been the opportunity to speak to one of them. It would have been out of the question in the visits hall and on the odd occasion there might have been the chance I had the feeling that wasn't done. It's certainly not encouraged which was a pity. I know they do a lot of locking and unlocking but it would have been helpful to know something of their training and exactly what their job entails. The most difficult question I was asked was,

Do you think what you are doing is worthwhile?

It has been for me, for different reasons. Whether any prisoner has found visits worthwhile, I wouldn't know. Mostly, they are men not used to communicating their feelings. They just talk generalities and I listen, responding where I can. I know when they have a visit it means they get off the wing, so there is a bit of a change in their daily lock and unlock life. There aren't many distractions for them, so I suppose it puts in an hour for them. I wouldn't think it changes their life in any way although I feel it has changed mine. Some of them ask for a visitor since they have neither family or friends who come to see them, so I think the bottom line is that a prison visitor is better than no one at all.

What is their room like? someone asked me. The use of the word 'room' for cell was the most naïve question I was asked. Or maybe not, since why should it be otherwise when, since as far as my straw poll went and any reference I have had on prison life, the lack of interest in the subject explains it. Anyway, here's how I described it.

The cells are small whether single or double. The windows are small and there are bars on them. There are bunk beds, a small table and somewhere to keep their clothes. The toilet is often just set apart with a curtain round it. I have spoken to prisoners who have been in establishments where there was still 'slopping out'.

They do have a TV. And pay 50p a week for it. This comes out of the £2.50 allocated to each prisoner. Who decides what to watch and at what time of the day can be a problem. Some like to watch into the night while others want to sleep at that time. Some prisoners keep them as scrupulously clean as possible. Others not so. Sharing with someone who is indifferent to keeping their cell clean is very hard on someone who is. Easy to see why a cell on your own is preferable in these circumstances. Some men used to keeping fit on the outside try finding a space at least to do press-ups.

A prisoner given a new cell, generally, has some cleaning out to do. Some say sharing is better since there is someone to talk to. Others prefer their own company, especially if they have experience of sharing with a difficult customer. Meals are taken in their cells and not in any kind of dining room. It might be different in other establishments but that's my experience of where I visited.

That's a lot of sharing between two grown men who know nothing about each other until they are banged up together. When your idea of prison life is gleaned from TV dramas or cinema, it's hard to describe what the reality is like. From what I've been told, it's mostly boring. The 'same old, same old' phrase applies more to prison life than any they have been used to on the outside.

Chapter 58

So how do prisoners manage their money in prison? The thing is they don't. The prison does, operating in a way like a bank. This is how that works. What money is theirs, the £2.50 from the prison goes on to what is known as their 'canteen'. If they have family or friends who send them money, they don't actually see that. Its handled by the prison and put into their account. That can be spent on toiletries, tea, coffee, biscuits, etc. to supplement what they have on their daily diet. Any item which is alcohol based would not be on their sheet. Each week, the prisoner receives this sheet saying what money he has, he fills out what he wants and that then comes to his cell. I was told on one of my visits what this is like for him.

"I see the number of things some guy has ordered and I'm on the basic. That's when it hurts. Makes me feel bitter about my family. They could help. They just don't care."

Since they have three meals a day and are provided with the bare essentials like toiletries, it could be said they don't actually need money but that's a basic existence. With maybe one or two exceptions, the men I visited, generally, had some money or clothes sent into them. Being able to buy better tea, coffee, or toiletries is a boon. It means something to look forward to in the week. There is no doubt that the men who receive nothing from outside find life very hard indeed.

I can only think of two, or possibly three of the men I have visited over the years who came from what could be described as 'a good background'. They were the exception. From my experience, the majority had an identikit background and life experience. A broken home, fostering, various Homes, sleeping rough or temporary shelter from friends and then prison was the norm for the men I saw.

Chapter 59

Visits can go wrong. The system for setting them up is not fool proof. Once given the prisoner's name and number, a date is set for the visit. It can happen that the prisoner has been released or transferred to another prison suddenly so the visitor has a wasted journey. In prison, things can change without warning. Letting the visitor know is not a top priority. It could be that the prisoner you plan to meet is 'down the block' a kind of solitary to keep him away from other inmates for one reason or another. A visit there is obviously out of the question.

Only twice have I been wrong-footed on a visit. First was with an inmate who thought I was a social worker who could give him practical help. I don't know how that could have happened and I felt terrible for him. There was nothing I could do except bring the 'visit' to an end.

The other was with Jason. Visiting him was an education and in some way, quite entertaining. He had not asked for an official visitor and for some reason, presumed it was one of his family who was visiting. He didn't seem too disappointed when I explained I was an official visitor. On the contrary, it gave him a captive audience for a lecture since according to Jason, there were flaws in the criminal justice system and in prisons generally. The Prison Service, as I was about to learn, was one of his hobby horses. There were flaws, he kept insisting, which should be corrected.

"In a funny kind of a way, being in here gives me a first-hand experience of what's wrong," he said.

He told me he was in business but couldn't divulge too much about it. I couldn't imagine what kind of business he was in or what his offence was. His manner was quite genial and he seemed unperturbed that I wasn't what he had expected. I had no idea how that could have gone wrong but didn't admit that to Jason. I didn't want to give him any more ammunition for his lecture on what's wrong about prison. He was a bit like a successful salesman sharing his expertise with someone less successful than him.

I could have explained my predicament to an officer but decided against it. Jason was such an unusual one-off it seemed a pity to stop him. My part was just to nod, and smile every now and then until visiting time was up.

I bumped into another visitor on the way out who asked how my visit went.

"Hard to say, really. I think he enjoyed it all right."

Chapter 60

The Catholic chaplain asked if I could come in on a Saturday morning. This was unconnected with my usual Monday evening visiting. He explained that one of the men on E wing wanted to become a Catholic and had been taking instruction in the faith for a year.

"He just wants someone apart from a priest listening to him. You're just the one," he assured me.

I was used to listening but something like this seemed out with my remit. It didn't sound like an ordinary visit.

I was told that this man had been sure for a long time this is what he wanted. He had done a great deal of reading and was completely committed.

It was an unusual idea but I couldn't really say no. I was used to listening and I didn't see that it could do any harm

Gerard was a very serious, unsmiling young man. He didn't make any general conversation, but it was clear he was in no doubt as to what he was doing. He just told me he had been receiving instruction in the faith and hoped to be received into the Catholic Church in a few weeks. He brought some of the books he had been studying in with him. Apart from saying that his father had offered to have him back home, that was his only general conversation. It was a long hour.

I did a Saturday morning stint with him for three weeks and they followed the same pattern. Once he was received into the church, the chaplain invited me to a little celebration for Gerard shortly afterwards. Tea and biscuits were laid on in the Chapel and one or two of the men he knew were invited. They looked genuinely pleased for him. My part in it was minimal and could have added nothing to what studying he had done.

I was glad Gerard had got to what he wanted but it was a novel kind of visiting for me.

Chapter 61

Trevor had been given a chance to see the outside world for a day so I had an idea of how our next visit would go. It was bound to be hard for him so I knew I should sit tight and just listen. Normally, I did all the talking since Trevor was a man of few words, but not this time. He had been let out in the company of two officers to attend his brother's funeral and it had been much harder than he expected. Since I already knew that his brother had never visited and there was not much of a bond between them anyway, I couldn't imagine how that day must have felt.

"There were so many of my family there and a couple of my brother's mates but none of them looked at me. I tried not to look over at them. The officers stood alongside me. We were kind of on the edge of things. Maybe they thought I might kick off. I was afraid people would see me in handcuffs but the officers took them off when we got out of the car. It didn't last long so I just tried to keep my head down. I was in the car, cuffs back on again before I knew it."

That was the first time I had heard Trevor speak at any length. There was nothing I could say, except to mumble, 'I'm so sorry' but he never reacted. It was more like a monologue than anything else.

"I expect it was hard for everyone," I said which wasn't very helpful but it made him take up the story again. I was relieved in a way since sitting with him in silence would have been worse.

"I expect they went to the Travellers afterwards." That was his old pub.

"I didn't know what the funeral would be like. I didn't think it would be like that. Never thought I'd be glad to get back in here again."

There seemed nothing else to say. I mumbled 'I'm so sorry' a couple of times. I couldn't imagine how that day must have been for him. I certainly couldn't think of anything that would help so we sat in silence until the officer came to take him back to his Wing.

Trevor didn't come over for his next visit or the one after. According to the chaplain, he was in a bit of trouble but didn't expand on that. I was sorry in a way since I knew I should have done better on our visit. Maybe I could say something useful to him this time. Or maybe not. He had looked so stricken recalling the funeral details it seemed to have got past words.

I knew he was in and out of this prison regularly as well as other establishments so maybe his family had just got tired of him. The funeral must have been hard for them too, seeing Trevor in the company of prison officers. I didn't know their side of the story. Trevor had only once referred to his lack of visits but he certainly sounded bitter about it. I don't know why he should get involved in trouble on the wing so soon after the funeral. Maybe he was just getting something out of his system but I never got the chance to find out. As with all my visits, I never learned whether here was a happy or a sad ending to their stories.

Chapter 62

If the press is to be believed, the public is fascinated by accounts of 'life inside'. A random sample from one National daily would be something like this – Prisoners who want the right to vote, inmates who can no longer be sent books to read, are held in top security prisons when their offence calls for an open, are held in poor conditions in a privately run prison, are deprived from following study courses and so on.

Different accounts with different agendas depending on which newspaper you are reading. You might say we are bombarded with information. It gets hard to see how you can pick your way through it all.

So the public are well informed on what it's like inside? Not so, since media stories have to focus on what's newsworthy. The more lurid tabloid accounts concentrate on the extraordinary. As a prison visitor for the last ten years, I have had a good insight into the 'ordinary' through weekly talks with prisoners. These are not stories which would hit the headlines. But in my ten years stint of weekly visits, I have been given a more realistic idea of a prisoner's life.

The biggest problem for prisoners about to be released can be summed up in one word – housing. It's not a subject covered in any length by the press but I would be hard pressed to think of one inmate who has told me that he has no problem with that. As far as housing goes, the best the majority of inmates have to look forward to is a temporary space in a mate's flat, a hostel or rough sleeping. That temporary space is more likely to be a pipe dream, hostels provide a fair chance of getting them on to drugs, if they are not already users and the increase in rough sleeping continues to rise. Parole Boards have to deal with this problem constantly. They interview a prisoner who is deemed no longer necessary to be kept in prison. He is judged ready for release since he no longer poses a threat to the public but the Board then faces the problem. Where is this man going to live when he walks out of the gate? Decent single homeless provision is needed for them but at this point that doesn't look like a priority

What I have learned as a prison visitor won't be found in newspaper accounts. It's more interesting than that because it's day-to-day prison life as it really is. It's more a slice of life, prison life, sometimes sad, sometimes uplifting and sometimes oddly rewarding. This is not one the public will learn from newspaper stories.

The man in the street will still prefer his own take on prison life. Ten years of talking to – and listening to men inside told me a different story.